INSIGHTS

2024

Junko Murao   Akiko Miyama   Tomoko Tsujimoto
Kana Yokoyama   Christopher Cladis

JN125961

KINSEIDO

Kinseido Publishing Co., Ltd.

3-21 Kanda Jimbo-cho, Chiyoda-ku,
Tokyo 101-0051, Japan

First published 2024 by Kinseido Publishing Co., Ltd.

Editorial support: C-leps Co., Ltd.

音声ファイル無料ダウンロード

https://www.kinsei-do.co.jp/download/4192

この教科書で 🔽 DL 00 の表示がある箇所の音声は、上記 URL または QR コードにて無料でダウンロードできます。自習用音声としてご活用ください。

▶ PC からのダウンロードをお勧めします。スマートフォンなどでダウンロードされる場合は、ダウンロード前に「解凍アプリ」をインストールしてください。

▶ URL は、検索ボックスではなくアドレスバー (URL 表示覧) に入力してください。

▶ お使いのネットワーク環境によっては、ダウンロードできない場合があります。

◎ CD 00　左記の表示がある箇所の音声は、教室用 CD（Class Audio CD）に収録されています。

　昨今話題のChatGPTといった生成AIの登場によって、人間の在り方だけでなく、教育の在り方も変化を余儀なくされています。従来に増して、情報を正確に読み取り、正しい情報を見極める能力が必要とされるようになると思われます。その意味では、できるだけ多くの事柄をある程度知っておくことは必要であるかもしれません。このテキストでは、教育・医療・経済・文化・環境・技術・社会・生物・農業・科学・テクノロジーといった幅広い分野のさまざまなトピックの記事を読みながら、生きた英語を学び、広い視野を養えるようになっています。また、各章の話題は、ディスカッションのトピックとしてもご利用いただけます。本テキストを授業内でのさまざまな活動にお役立ていただければと思います。

━━● Key Expressions 1

　写真などの視覚情報を見てトピックへの関心を促す、リーディング・セクション読解のためのキーワードのブランク埋めの問題です。キーワードを耳で聞くだけでなく、最初の一文字と語数をヒントにして、辞書も参照しながら解答してみてください。リーディング・セクションの背景知識を構築しながら、辞書を用いて文法も確認する練習問題となっています。

━━● Key Expressions 2

　リーディング・セクション中に登場する重要表現や、TOEIC® Testsにも出現頻度の高い語彙を学習するエクササイズです。単なるキーワードの意味理解だけでなく、関連語句や派生語を構成する接頭辞・接尾辞の意味など、単語力増強に必要な情報が盛り込まれています。

━━● Key Expressions 3

　話題に関連した構文や語法の練習問題です。基礎的な文法力も試せる問題となっています。

━━● Background Knowledge

　リーディング・セクションの背景を構築する短い記事を読み、簡単な速読用の設問を解きます。一語一句訳すのではなく、必要な情報のみを拾い読みするという速読方法（スキャニング）で読んでみてください。語彙の類推力を養うために、辞書を参照せずに解答してみましょう。

━━● Newspaper English

　文法確認のセクションです。網羅的に文法を扱ってはいませんが、英文記事を読むために最低限必要な文法の基礎知識や表現ルールを学びます。

━━● Reading

　本セクションを読むまでに、かなりの背景知識・文法・語彙の構築ができています。ここまでのセクションをしっかり復習しておけば、辞書なしでもほぼ理解できるでしょう。読解の助けになる注は付けていますが、できるだけ注を参照しないで読むよう心がけてください。

━━● Comprehension, Summary

　リーディング・セクションの内容が理解できているかどうかのチェックを行います。

━━● Insights into Today's World

　リーディング・セクションの記事で取り上げられているトピックに関して、自分の意見を述べる練習をします。与えられている質問をもとに、まずは英語で自分の意見を書いてから、クラスメイトと意見交換をしてみましょう。

　以上のようなバラエティに富んだ練習問題によって、英字新聞やインターネットのニュース記事を抵抗感なく読めるようになるはずです。最後になりましたが、テキスト作成の際にお世話になりました金星堂編集部の皆様に心からお礼を申し上げます。

編著者

● 英字新聞を知ろう ●

　英字新聞を目の前にすると、一体どこからどのように読んでいけばよいのか迷う人もいるでしょう。まずは、以下のジャパンタイムズ紙のフロントページ（第一面）やジャパンニューズ紙のオンライン版トップページを見ながら、英字新聞を読む際に知っておくべきことを学びましょう。大きなニュースは繰り返しフロントページで取り上げられることがあります。まずはこのページで、持続性があり、興味を持てる話題を選択し、しばらくそのニュースを追いかけていく読み方がお勧めです。同じ話題のニュースに何度も触れていると、次第に辞書なしで読めるようになるでしょう。

１．紙媒体のフロントページの構成

新聞社のロゴ（Logo）

これは紙媒体のジャパンタイムズ紙のフロントページです。ジャパンタイムズ紙は、ニューヨークタイムズ紙とセットでも販売されており、国内・海外の情報を幅広く提供しています。

重要記事の紹介

各紙面から大きなニュースを取り上げ簡単に紹介しています。

ヘッドライン（Headline）

ヘッドラインの詳しい説明は p.6 参照。

リード（Lead）

記事の書き出しの一段落目のことをリードと呼びます。ニュースの概略が紹介されます。リードには、5Ws1Hの情報ができるだけ盛り込まれます。

キャプション（Caption）

図版や写真に付く説明文のことです。記事を読むときの大切な背景知識を提供しています。先に目を通しておくと記事の理解の助けとなります。

目次

記事のジャンルと掲載ページが提示されます。

２．オンライン版のトップページ

新聞社のロゴ（Logo）

これは読売新聞の英語版ジャパンニューズ紙のトップページです。紙媒体とは異なり、文字数を減らし、視覚情報の多い作りとなっています。ヘッドラインをクリックすると記事全体が読めます。

記事のカテゴリー

各項目をクリックすると、政治・社会・ビジネス・スポーツなど、カテゴリー別に記事を日をさかのぼって読むことができます。

トップニュース
（Top News）

紙媒体でいうフロントページに載る重要記事が紹介されます。

その他の重要記事や特集の紹介

３．ヘッドラインの特徴 ───────────────

① 記事を新鮮に見せるために動詞の過去・現在完了が現在形で表されることが多い

Strong earthquake strikes Japan's Kumamoto「強い地震が日本の熊本を襲う」

② 「進行形・近接未来」や「受動態」では be 動詞が省略され、それぞれ V-ing や V-ed の形で表される

Virtual spaces coaxing Japan's social recluses back into society　「ヴァーチャルな空間が日本のひきこもりの人々を社会復帰するよう促している」(*The Japan Times*, April 13, 2023)

Russian TV protester listed as wanted fugitive　「ロシアのTV抗議者指名手配中の亡命者としてリストに載る」(*Reuters*, October 4, 2022)

③ 未来は不定詞 (to V) で表されることが多い

Biden to visit Japan　「バイデン大統領日本を訪問予定」

④ 冠詞や be 動詞は省略されることが多い

Book store owner in Hyogo laments the passing of an era　「兵庫県の本屋のオーナー時代の変遷を悲しむ」

Missing part of Japan's 1st imported novel found in Osaka　「日本初の輸入小説の不明箇所大阪で見つかる」(*The Asahi Shimbun*, August 31, 2022)

⑤ 情報源を示すためにコロン (：) を用いることがある

Survey: Over 60% constantly keep masks on「調査によると60％以上の人が常にマスク着用」(*Jiji Press*, April 27, 2023)

⑥ 省略や略語が多用される

gov't → government（政府）　　pref. → prefecture（県）

fest → festival（フェスティバル、祭り）

int'l → international（国際的な）

MPD → The Metropolitan Police Department（警視庁）

SDF → The Self-Defense Force（自衛隊）

⑦ **カンマによって and が省略される**

Emperor, Empress visit Tokyo firm hiring many disabled people「天皇皇后両陛下が障害を持つ人を多く雇用している東京の企業を訪問」

⑧ **短い綴りの語が好まれる**

eye「目指す、狙う」 ink「署名する」 vie「張り合う、競争する」
nix「拒否する、禁止する」

4．英字新聞攻略法

さて、新聞全体の構成が分かったところで、どのように英字新聞に親しんでいけばよいのでしょうか。

① 英字新聞の言語的特徴に慣れよう

英字新聞は、**3．ヘッドラインの特徴**で見たように、ニュースを新鮮に見せるためにヘッドラインを現在形で書くなど、読者を引きつけるさまざまな工夫がなされています。本書では、その工夫に関して **Newspaper English** のセクションで取り上げていますので、問題を解答しながらまずその特徴を覚えましょう。

② すべての記事を読む必要はない

すべての記事を隅々まで読むのは大変ですし、その必要もありません。まずは、ヘッドラインや写真などを見て、興味のある記事だけを読んでみましょう。英字新聞に慣れるまでは、できるだけ日本に関する記事を選ぶほうが読みやすいでしょう。

③ 背景知識を提供するリード・写真・キャプションは、最初に目を通そう

記事（特にニュース記事）の本文は、リードに最重要情報が置かれ、パラグラフが進むにつれ情報の重要度が下がっていきますから、しばらくはリードだけに挑戦するのもよいでしょう。

④ 特定のテーマに絞って読むようにしよう

特定のテーマを継続して読む方法が英語学習には最適です。あるテーマに特有の語彙をまとめて学習することができるので、類似テーマの記事なら簡単に読めるようになるからです。

Insights 2024 Table of Contents

Hug a Seal, Begin to Heal

なぜか癒してくれるアザラシ

Ukrainian children fleeing to Poland pet PARO (Provided by Mazovian Neuropsychiatric Center in Warsaw, Poland)

Key Expressions 1

🎧 DL 02　　◎ CD 1-02

音声を聞いて1〜3の（　　）内に適当な語を書き入れましょう。

1. PARO is one of the world's most successful (t _ _ _ _ _ _ _ _ _ _) robots.

   パロは、世界で最も成功しているセラピーロボットのひとつである。

2. The robot is so popular that some (r _ _ _ _) to it as "Japan's pride."

   そのロボットはあまりに人気なので、「日本の誇り」と言う人もいる。

3. Its artificial intelligence programming enables it to recognize its (s _ _ _ _ _ _ _ _ _ _ _)

   and respond to being touched with corresponding sounds.

   人工知能のプログラミングにより、それ（パロ）は周辺のものを認識し、触れられるとふさわしい音で
   反応することができる。

Key Expressions 2

1 〜 5 はセラピーロボットパロに関連する語です。選択肢 a 〜 e より英英定義を選び、さらに日本語の意味を [　　] 内に書き入れましょう。

1. fluffy　　　　　（　）　[　　　　　　　　　　　]
2. squeak　　　　（　）　[　　　　　　　　　　　]
3. adorable　　　（　）　[　　　　　　　　　　　]
4. tactile　　　　（　）　[　　　　　　　　　　　]
5. whiskers　　　（　）　[　　　　　　　　　　　]

> a. a short, very high cry or sound
> b. soft like wool or fur
> c. long hairs that grow near an animal's mouth
> d. related to the sense of touch
> e. charming, attractive, and easy to love

Key Expressions 3

受動態〈be 動詞 + 過去分詞〉は「〜される」という意味を持ちます。1 〜 3 の英文の（　　）内の動詞もしくは副詞を含む動詞を受動態にして、英文を完成させましょう。時制や、副詞を伴うものはその位置にも注意しましょう。

1. After the first-generation PARO (complete →　　　　　　　　　　　) in 1998, improvements, such as a reduction in weight, (continuously make →　　　　　　　　　　　).
   第一世代のパロが 1998 年に完成した後、軽量化のような改良が継続してなされた。

2. While real animals (often prohibit →　　　　　　　　　　) from medical centers and seniors' homes, the antimicrobial features of PARO's artificial hair mean that it can even stay with patients in intensive care units.
   本物の動物は医療センターや老人ホームからはよく禁止されるが、パロの人工毛の抗菌性の特徴は、集中治療室にいる患者とでも一緒にいられるということである。

3. Eighty units (send →　　　　　　　　　　) to evacuation centers and elsewhere in the aftermath of the 2011 Great East Japan Earthquake and tsunami to help survivors.
   2011 年の東日本大震災と津波の後、生存者を助けるために避難所やその他の場所に 80 体（のパロロボット）が届けられた。

Background Knowledge

CD 1-03

セラピーロボット・パロの制作者である柴田崇徳氏の研究について、英文に述べられていないものを1〜4から選びましょう。

　In the United States, animal therapy had been a subject of formal academic research for three decades, and Shibata soon learned it had been used to help everyone from cancer patients to children with developmental disabilities.

　Shibata created three prototypes modeled on a dog, cat and seal, and gave them to MIT students to try out. They were most excited about the dog and cat, but most ended up ranking them lower than the seals, Shibata said. For some foreign students, the reason seemed cultural. They knew less about seals, so they came with fewer preconceptions.

The Asahi Shimbun

Note　MIT（Massachusetts Institute of Technology）「マサチューセッツ工科大学」

1. 米国ではすでに30年前からアニマルセラピーの研究が行われていた。
2. 柴田氏は、米国で癌患者から発達障害の子どもまであらゆる人を助けるためにアニマルセラピーが行われていることを知った。
3. 柴田氏は、犬と猫とアザラシをモデルにした試作品をMITの学生に作ってもらった。
4. セラピーロボットの模型を体験したMITの学生は、アザラシをランキングのトップに選んだ。

Newspaper English

英文新聞では、記事を限られたスペースに収めるために語句を省略する場合が多々あります。副詞節を導く接続詞（while, when, if）の後ろに続くフレーズの主語とbe動詞は、しばしば省略されます。

以下の1と2の文章の下線部を、省略されている語句を補った形で（　　）内に書き入れましょう。

1. The robotic seals can remember their nicknames and react to them <u>when called</u>.
　　　　　　　　　　　　（　　　　　　　　　　　　　　　　　　）
　そのロボットのアザラシは、ニックネームを覚え、呼ばれたらそれに反応することができる。

2. And <u>if kept</u> long enough, they even eventually develop their own habits.
　（　　　　　　　　　　　　　　　　　　）
　そして、十分長い期間所持されると、それらは最終的に独自の癖を身につけたりもする。

Reading

Adorable robot therapy seal helps relieve anxiety, stress

relieve... 「〜を緩和する」

TSUKUBA, Ibaraki Prefecture—In a lab tightly packed with models of therapy robots, a harp seal with light pink hair looks up at the person stroking its fluffy head and lets out an affectionate squeak.

harp seal 「タテゴトアザラシ」
looked up at... 「〜を見上げる」
affectionate 「優しい」

5　This is PARO, one of the world's most successful therapeutic robots—popular to the extent that some refer to it as "Japan's pride."

to the extent... 「〜の程度まで」

"I came up with the idea for a pet robot because I thought consumers would welcome machines that do not do home 10 chores like washing clothes and cleaning rooms," said its creator, Takanori Shibata, a top researcher at the National Institute of Advanced Industrial Science and Technology.

chores 「雑用」
the National Institute of Advanced Industrial Science and Technology 「国立研究開発法人産業技術総合研究所」

The seal's body, whiskers and nose are outfitted with visual, tactile and auditory sensors. Using artificial 15 intelligence, it can recognize its surroundings and respond to being touched with corresponding sounds.

be outfitted with... 「〜がついている、備わっている」

The robotic seals can remember their nicknames and react to them when called. And if kept long enough, they even eventually develop their own habits.

20　If that sounds more like a pet than a robot, that is because it was designed to make patients feel calm and content.

Clinical research shows that when people suffering from dementia hold and speak to PARO, it can make their peripheral symptoms milder, providing benefits similar to 25 animal therapy.

dementia 「認知症」
peripheral symptoms 「(暴言、徘徊といった、認知障害にとどまらない) 周辺症状」

One U.S. study showed a drop in anxiety that allowed doctors to cut their patients' intake of psychotropic drugs by 30 percent. And miraculously, the robot produces effects that last more than two hours longer than the drugs.

psychotropic drugs 「向精神薬」

30　In Britain, PARO is included in a governmental organization's guidelines for non-drug dementia treatment options covered by public health insurance.

public health insurance 「公的健康保険」

The first PARO was made in 1998. Succeeding generations of the robot were made to test improvements. By the eighth-35 generation PARO, it was ready for mass production. The

eighth-generation「第 8 世代の」

latest model, the ninth, is still not cheap. It carries a price tag of 450,000 yen ($3,200), though it costs nearly twice as much outside Japan.

But the benefits seem to have made the high cost worth it.　worth it「それだけの価値のある」
40 While real animals are often prohibited in medical centers and homes of senior citizens, the antimicrobial features of PARO's artificial hair mean that it can even stay with patients in intensive care units.

Robot owners also do not suffer the devastation of losing a　devastation「感情的な打撃」
45 beloved pet.

PARO can go anywhere safely. Officials sent 80 units to evacuation centers and elsewhere in the aftermath of the 2011 Great East Japan Earthquake and tsunami to help survivors cope.　cope「乗り越える」

The Asahi Shimbun

● Comprehension

本文の内容に合うように、1と3の英文を完成させるのに適当なものを、2の質問の答えとして適当なものをa～dから選びましょう。

1. Takanori Shibata believes that consumers

  a. are unwilling to pay a high price for a pet robot.

  b. prefer robots that can help with tasks around the house.

  c. will prefer pet robots with vibrant colors, such as pink.

  d. are open to the presence of new types of machines in their homes.

2. Which of the following is NOT a feature of Takanori Shibata's robotic seals?

  a. Three types of sensors can be found on the body, whiskers and nose.

  b. Using artificial intelligence, they can call their owners by their nicknames.

  c. They can perceive the environment around them and respond accordingly.

  d. When appropriate, they make various sounds, such as squeaking.

3. According to the research, PARO, the therapeutic robot seal,

  a. can relieve symptoms of dementia if patients hold and speak to it for more than two hours.

  b. can reduce anxiety levels in patients by up to 30 percent.

  c. affects patients in a way that is comparable to animal therapy.

  d. is most effective when paired with psychotropic drugs during treatment.

Summary

以下の空所 1 ～ 4 に当てはまる語句を選択肢から選び、書き入れましょう。

> With its ninth model currently on the market, PARO, the (1.　　　　　　　　　　) robot seal is being used to treat patients throughout the world, including those suffering from dementia and anxiety. With its (2.　　　　　　　　　　) technology, including a variety of sensors and artificial intelligence, along with its animal-like behavior and general cuteness, PARO is a (3.　　　　　　　　　　) yet powerful tool for doctors to utilize. Research even shows that with PARO, doctors can reduce the amount of (4.　　　　　　　　　　) drugs they use to treat their patients.

psychotropic　　simple　　therapeutic　　sophisticated

Insights into Today's World

🎧 DL 04　◎ CD 1-06

以下の対話の空所に、あなたのアイデアを書いてみましょう。その後、クラスメイトにその内容を伝えてみましょう。

> I have heard about therapeutic robots, but I couldn't imagine what they were like. This robot is so cute that I would surely be healed by it if I was ever in need. Animals are said to have healing power. I am surprised to hear that even a robot has such power. **Do you think you would like to use PARO?**

For me, _____

_____

Chapter 02

Inheriting Traditional Sounds

日本の伝統的な音を継承するために

From left, shamisen, one each using synthetic leather, cat skin, kangaroo skin, and dog skin (The Mainichi)

● Key Expressions 1

🎧 DL 05   ◎ CD 1-07

音声を聞いて 1 〜 3 の（　　）内に適当な語を書き入れましょう。

1. The shamisen industry faces a dilemma of having to decide between preserving
   (t _ _ _ _ _ _ _ _) and protecting animals.
   三味線業界は、伝統を守ることと動物を保護することの間で決断しなければならないというジレンマに
   直面している。

2. The use of animal skins for the production of shamisen came to be
   (c _ _ _ _ _ _ _ _ _).
   三味線に動物の皮を使うことは、批判されるようになった。

3. A concert featuring shamisen made with washi paper was (h _ _ _) in Kyoto.
   和紙を使って作られた三味線を呼び物にした演奏会が、京都で開催された。

Key Expressions 2

副詞の多くは、形容詞の語尾に ly を付けて作ります。形容詞の語尾にそのまま ly や y を付けるパターンや、形容詞の語尾の y を i に変えて ly を付けるパターンがあります。

1 〜 5 の日本語の意味に合うように、選択肢の形容詞を副詞の形に変えて（　　）内に書き入れましょう。

1. 伝統的に　　　　　　　　　（　　　　　　　　　　　　　　）
2. 絶妙に　　　　　　　　　　（　　　　　　　　　　　　　　）
3. 一時的に　　　　　　　　　（　　　　　　　　　　　　　　）
4. 専門的には　　　　　　　　（　　　　　　　　　　　　　　）
5. 明白に　　　　　　　　　　（　　　　　　　　　　　　　　）

exquisite　professional　apparent　traditional　temporary

Key Expressions 3

大きな数を英語で読む場合のルールとして、以下を覚えておきましょう。

・桁の大きな数：「下 3 桁ごと」にコンマで区切り、3 桁のところで thousand、6 桁のところで million と単位を付けます。→ 100,000,000
　　　　　　　　　　　　　　　　　　↑　　　↑
　　　　　　　　　　　　　million　thousand

・西暦：前半と後半の 2 桁ずつに分けて読みます。「2010 年以降」の西暦については、thousand を使って読むパターンもあります。また、2000 年〜 2009 年では two thousand nine のように thousand を使うことが一般的です。

1 と 2 の下線部の数字の読み方を、例のようにつづりで書きましょう。

例：There are 84 musical instrument stores in this city.（ eighty-four ）

1. The number of shamisen manufactured was 3,400 at that time.

   （　　　　　　　　　　　　　　　　　　　　　　　　　　　　　　　　　　）

2. The Agency for Cultural Affairs launched a project in fiscal 2021.

   2 桁ずつ区切って読むパターン：

   （　　　　　　　　　　　　　　　　　　　　　　　　　　　　　　　　　　）

   thousand を使って読むパターン：

   （　　　　　　　　　　　　　　　　　　　　　　　　　　　　　　　　　　）

Background Knowledge

CD 1-08

早稲田大学の真辺将之教授のコメントについて、英文に<u>述べられていないもの</u>を 1 〜 4 から選びましょう。

Masayuki Manabe, a professor at Waseda University who has researched the history of relations between animals and humans, said that Japanese society in the Edo period and Meiji era did not place value on animal protection as much as people do now, and there were even individuals who ate cats amid food shortages during and after World War II.

After society became more prosperous following a period of rapid economic growth, the Act on Welfare and Management of Animals, which bans animal abuse, was adopted in 1973. Manabe pointed out that around this time, pets began to be adored as family members. He said, "The usage of cat skin for shamisen became subjected to stronger criticism and measures, such as the establishment of a group of victims united against dealers that capture cats."

The Mainichi

Note become subjected to... 「〜にさらされるようになる」

1. 江戸時代や明治時代の日本社会は、現在ほど動物保護に価値を置いていなかった。
2. 1973 年に、動物虐待を禁止する法律が制定された。
3. 高度経済成長期後も、ペットが家族として可愛がられる風潮はまだなかった。
4. 三味線に猫の皮が使われていることに、批判と対策が強まった。

Newspaper English

 新聞記事の見出し（ヘッドライン）では、冠詞や be 動詞が省略されることがあります。限られたスペース内で語数を減らし、読者にインパクトを与えるためです。

以下のヘッドラインに省略されている語を補って完全な文の形にし、また 1 〜 4 の空所を埋めて日本語訳を完成させなさい。

Shamisen industry in a pinch to protect unique sound integral to Japanese theater

→ (¹.   ) Shamisen industry (².   ) in a pinch to protect its unique sound, integral to Japanese theater.

日本語訳：三味線業界は、日本の演劇に欠かせない (³.   ) 音を
(⁴.   ) ため苦境に陥っている。

Reading

Shamisen industry in a pinch to protect unique sound integral to Japanese theater

Japan's "shamisen" industry is struggling to preserve the distinctive sound of the three-stringed instrument integral to Japanese performing arts, as it runs into issues of animal ethics and a decrease in the number of players.

5　Kotaro Tanaka heads Isamiya Hogakkiten, a traditional musical instrument shop in Hamada, Shimane Prefecture, which has also carried out the task of stretching hide over the shamisen's resonating body since the late 1970s. He said, "There is an uneven thickness to animal skin, which gives

10　rise to a depth in the sound. In particular, cat skin has an exquisite balance."

However, there was a decrease in supplies due to opposition from cat lovers and other activists, and in the 1980s, the shop began to depend on imported cat skin. Prices

15　surged as supplies fell, and though the shop used the skin of Southeast Asian dogs as a temporary substitute, these also became difficult to obtain from the standpoint of animal protection.

Synthetic leather tends to produce monotonous sounds,

20　and professional players avoid their usage on theatrical stages and in recitals. The shamisen industry strives to keep the tradition alive through endeavors such as a performance held in Kyoto in 2021 which featured shamisen using "washi" paper in place of animal skin.

25　The industry also faces the problem of a shrinking market. The number of shamisen manufactured in Japan fell from 18,000 in 1970 to 3,400 in 2017, according to the National Federation of Traditional Instrument Shops. A decrease in the number of people who play the instrument as a hobby

30　or for a living, such as during teahouse performances, was a factor behind the plummeting figure. To make matters worse, many musical concerts and theatrical productions in recent years were canceled amid the spread of the coronavirus.

35　Tanaka of Isamiya Hogakkiten said, "The sounds of

---

struggle「奮闘する」
distinctive「独特な」
run into...「～に直面する」

head...「～経営する」

hide「皮」
resonating body「共鳴胴」
give rise to...「～を生じさせる」

surge「高騰する」
substitute「代替品」
standpoint「観点」

synthetic「合成の」
monotonous「単調な」

endeavor「努力」

in place of...「～の代わりに」

teahouse「喫茶店」
plummeting「急落する」

instruments change with the times. However, we will
continue research to create shamisen that do not rely on
animal skins. I'd like people to know the charms of shamisen,
which can express a wide range of sounds, including sounds
40 full of vigor, and mellow, delicate notes."

rely on... 「～に頼る」

charm 「魅力」

vigor 「迫力」

mellow 「豊かな」

The Mainichi

参考

The National Federation of Traditional Instrument Shops「全国邦楽器組合連合会」

Comprehension

本文の内容に合うように、1 の英文を完成させるのに適当なものを、2 と 3 の質問の
答えとして適当なものを、a ～ d から選びましょう。

1. The operator of the traditional musical instrument shop, Isamiya Hogakkiten,
   a. started to depend on imported cat skin in the 1980s.
   b. relies on imported dog skin to produce shamisen.
   c. prefers domestic animal skin over the imported variety.
   d. endured a supply scarcity in the late 1970s.

2. Why do professional players tend not to prefer the use of shamisen made with
   synthetic leathers?
   a. They are more expensive than those made with animal skin.
   b. Audiences find their modern appearance inappropriate.
   c. They produce a monotonous sound that is not preferred by performers.
   d. Shamisen made using cat skin are more traditional.

3. Which of the following is NOT a problem the shamisen industry recently faced?
   a. The market has shrunk over the last several decades.
   b. Fewer people choose to make a living playing the instrument.
   c. Cancellation of events due to the coronavirus pandemic.
   d. The widespread closure of traditional teahouses.

Summary

🎧 DL 06　💿 CD 1-10

以下の空所 1 ～ 4 に当てはまる語を選択肢から選び、書き入れましょう。

Issues related to the ($^{1.}$　　　　　　　) treatment of animals and the dwindling population of players have left the shamisen industry struggling to find a place in the Japanese ($^{2.}$　　　　　　　) landscape. Opposition to the use of animal skin to manufacture the instrument has led to experimentation with ($^{3.}$　　　　　　　) materials, such as synthetic leather, which are not ideal. Additionally, the market has severely declined in ($^{4.}$　　　　　　　) decades as fewer people choose to take up the shamisen as a hobby or profession.

ethical　　alternative　　cultural　　recent

Insights into Today's World

🎧 DL 07　💿 CD 1-11

以下の対話の空所に、あなたの知識を書いてみましょう。その後、クラスメイトにその内容を伝えてみましょう。

In our daily life, we encounter various products made from animal skins. **Besides shamisen, what other products made from animal skin do we have in our lives?**

For example, _____
_____

Chapter 03
Used Home Appliances Gaining Popularity

中古家電が人気

Used home appliances showcased in a secondhand store (The Asahi Shimbun)

● **Key Expressions 1**

🎧 DL 08   ◎ CD 1-12

音声を聞いて 1 ～ 3 の（　　）内に適当な語を書き入れましょう。

1. Consumers have become less (n _ _ _ _ _ _ _) about used products.
   消費者が中古品に対して以前ほど否定的でなくなってきた。

2. A (l _ _ _ _ _ _) home electric appliance retailer made a foray into the secondhand market.
   ある大手家庭用電化製品の販売会社が中古市場に進出した。

3. Many customers buy them from brick-and-mortar secondhand (v _ _ _ _ _ _).
   中古品販売会社の実店舗でそれらを購入する客が多い。

Key Expressions 2

家電製品の英語名を学びましょう。1 ～ 6 の日本語に当てはまる語を選択肢から選び、
（　　）内に書き入れましょう。

1. 洗濯機　　　　　（　　　　　　　　　　　　　）
2. 掃除機　　　　　（　　　　　　　　　　　　　）
3. 加湿器　　　　　（　　　　　　　　　　　　　）
4. 食器洗浄機　　　（　　　　　　　　　　　　　）
5. エアコン　　　　（　　　　　　　　　　　　　）
6. 冷蔵庫　　　　　（　　　　　　　　　　　　　）

humidifier　　air conditioner　　dishwasher　　refrigerator

vacuum cleaner　　washing machine

Key Expressions 3

日本語訳を参考に、1 ～ 3 の英文の（　　　　　　）内に当てはまる副詞を選択肢から選び、
書き入れましょう。

1. The buying frenzy (　　　　　　　　　　　　　) subsided.
   購買熱は、次第に弱まった。

2. It is often the case that manufacturers raise the prices of their products
   (　　　　　　　　　　　　　) within a short period.
   メーカーが短期間に繰り返し自社製品の価格を上げる場合が多い。

3. Consumers are becoming (　　　　　　　　　　　　　) price-conscious.
   消費者はますます価格に敏感になりつつある。

repeatedly　　increasingly　　gradually

Background Knowledge

CD 1-13

株式会社ヤマダホールディングスの中古家電再生工場について、英文に述べられていないものを1～4から選びましょう。

Yamada Holdings Co. set up a recycling factory for used home appliances in Fujioka, Gunma Prefecture. The company buys used appliances from its customers when they purchase new ones or for other reasons. The used items are repaired, checked, and cleaned before they are shipped.

For instance, a refrigerator is evaluated on the basis of 24 categories, including whether it can ensure appropriate temperatures, according to the company.

The Asahi Shimbun

Notes　evaluate...「～を査定する」ensure...「～を確かにする、保証する」

1. 群馬県に新しい家電再生工場を建設する予定である。
2. 顧客が新品を購入する際などに中古家電を買い取る。
3. 再生工場では、中古品を修理、検査、洗浄してから出荷する。
4. 中古の冷蔵庫は24の項目に基づいて査定される。

Newspaper English

 英文記事では、ことわざを使うことで記事の内容を読者に印象づけることがあります。日本語にも似たことわざがある場合も少なくありません。ぜひいくつか覚えておきましょう。

1～3の英語のことわざに近い意味の日本のことわざを、選択肢から選びましょう。

1. One man's trash is another man's treasure.　（　　）

2. The early bird catches the worm.　（　　）

3. It's no use crying over spilled milk.　（　　）

> **a.** 早起きは三文の得　　**b.** 覆水盆に返らず　　**c.** 捨てる神あれば拾う神あり

Reading

Market for used home appliances undergoes a sea change in Japan

undergoes a sea change 「激変する」

The used electric appliance market in Japan is undergoing a boom as price-conscious consumers become less fussy about purchasing recycled products, giving weight to the saying that 'One man's trash is another man's treasure.'

price-conscious 「価格に敏感な」

fussy 「神経質な、細かいことにこだわる」

5 A 60-percent increase in such sales over the past five years is due in great measure to a worldwide semiconductor shortage that in turn triggered product shortages.

give weight to... 「～を重視する」

saying 「ことわざ、格言」

in great measure 「大いに」

semiconductor 「半導体」

Treasure Factory Co., which operates at least 150 secondhand stores mainly in the Kanto and Kansai regions, 10 has been going all-out to buy electric heaters, fan heaters and other winter home appliances.

in turn 「今度は、次に」

trigger... 「～を引き起こす」

go all-out to... 「総力を挙げて～する」

"We hope those who bought used home appliances during the summer will be interested in winter appliances as well," said Toshikazu Ozawa, an area manager for the company.

15 Air conditioners were the hot ticket item in the summer of 2022. In June, Treasure Factory sold 90 percent more units year on year, and almost went out of stock at one point. The buying frenzy gradually subsided. But in August, the company saw sales of washing machines grow by about 20 20 percent from a year earlier. Overall, sales of used home appliances increased by 12 percent year-on-year between January and August 2022.

hot ticket 「人気の物、人気者」

year on year 「前年比で」

go out of stock 「在庫切れ（売り切れ）になる」

Some secondhand electric appliances sell at nearly half the prices of new ones. "Prices for new products are expected 25 to continue to climb," Ozawa said. "With consumers becoming increasingly budget-minded, the number of people who buy used items is bound to increase further."

be expected to... 「～することが予想される」

climb 「上昇する」

budget-minded 「節約志向の」

be bound to... 「きっと～する、～する運命にある」

According to an estimate released by industry magazine, The Reuse Business Journal, the overall secondhand market 30 was worth about 2.7 trillion yen in 2021, with a year-on-year increase of 11.7 percent.

estimate 「推計」

industry magazine 「業界誌」

worth 「～相当の」

Of the total figure, the market for home appliances and furniture was worth 251.8 billion yen, a year-on-year increase of 6.2 percent.

of the total figure 「総額のうち、総額から」

35 The market continues to expand each year, and it has

expand 「拡大する」

grown by more than 60 percent from five years ago.

    Many customers looking for used home appliances and furniture shy away from marketplace apps and buy them from brick-and-mortar secondhand vendors because large-
40 sized furniture and household appliances require packaging and other delivery tasks.

The Asahi Shimbun

shy away from... 「～を敬遠する」

marketplace app 「フリーマーケットのアプリ」

packaging 「梱包」

delivery 「配送」

task 「仕事、作業」

● Comprehension

本文の内容に合うように、1の質問の答えとして適当なものを、2と3の英文を完成させるのに適当なものを、a ～ d から選びましょう。

1. Which is NOT one of the reasons for the boom in the used electric appliance market in Japan?
   a. There was a sudden surplus of discarded appliances.
   b. Consumers are more open to using such products.
   c. There was a scarcity of semiconductors worldwide.
   d. Consumers are managing their finances more carefully.

2. Secondhand store operator, Treasure Factory Co.
   a. saw a 90 percent increase in sales of washing machines in August.
   b. is preparing for an increase in the demand for summer home appliances.
   c. sold their entire stock of air conditioners last June.
   d. experienced a 12 percent increase in used home appliance sales in the first eight months of the year.

3. The sales in the secondhand market for home appliances and furniture
   a. are mostly made at actual stores, as opposed to online marketplaces.
   b. expanded by 11.7 percent from the previous year.
   c. are expected to drop in the coming years.
   d. increased by 60 percent annually over the last five years.

Summary

🎧 DL 09 　◎ CD 1-15

以下の空所1〜4に当てはまる語を選択肢から選び、書き入れましょう。

Spurred by product (1.　　　　　　　　　　　), as well as shifting attitudes, the Japanese market for used electric appliances has expanded substantially over the last several years. Seasonal (2.　　　　　　　　　　　), such as heaters and air conditioners, are particularly popular among budget-minded consumers who pay significantly lower (3.　　　　　　　　　) at secondhand stores. Such stores are likely to see (4.　　　　　　　　　) increase further, with prices for new products predicted to continue rising in coming years.

items　　prices　　shortages　　sales

Insights into Today's World

🎧 DL 10 　◎ CD 1-16

以下の対話の空所に、あなたのアイデアを書いてみましょう。その後、クラスメイトにその内容を伝えてみましょう。

As price hikes continue for everything we buy, used products will gain popularity. **Is there anything you think we should be careful about when we buy secondhand appliances?**

That's a good question! _____

_____

Chapter 04

The Ideal Solid Fuel

夢の固形燃料への転換

Biocoke made from plant materials (Provided by Kindai University)

Key Expressions 1

🎧 DL 11　◉ CD 1-17

音声を聞いて 1 〜 3 の（　　）内に適当な語を書き入れましょう。

1. Biocoke is one of the fuels that can (f _ _ _ _ _ _ _ _ _) the transition to a decarbonized society.

   バイオコークスは、脱炭素化社会への移行を促進するための燃料の一つである。

2. The cost of producing biocoke has fallen to a (r _ _ _ _ _ _ _ _ _) level.

   バイオコークスの製造コストは、妥当な水準まで下がってきた。

3. We aim to shift from using fossil resources to (r _ _ _ _ _ _ _ _) energy.

   私たちは、化石資源の使用から再生可能なエネルギーへの転換を目標にしている。

Key Expressions 2

動詞には規則的に変化する「規則動詞」と、不規則に変化する「不規則動詞」があります。
前者は「play-played-played」と、動詞の後ろに -ed をつけるだけで過去形・過去分詞形を
作ることが出来ますが、後者は活用の仕方が不規則なのでしっかり覚えておきましょう。

以下の不規則動詞（原形）の過去形と過去分詞形を（　　）内に書き入れましょう。

1. make　　―　　(　　　　　　　　　) ― (　　　　　　　　　)
2. get　　　―　　(　　　　　　　　　) ― (　　　　　　　　　)
3. be　　　―　　(　　　　　　　　　) ― (　　　　　　　　　)
4. build　　―　　(　　　　　　　　　) ― (　　　　　　　　　)
5. burn　　―　　(　　　　　　　　　) ― (　　　　　　　　　)

Key Expressions 3

日本語訳を参考に、1〜3の（　　）内に当てはまる語句を選択肢から選び、必要で
あれば形を変えて書き入れましょう。

1. The research continues to (　　　　　　　　　　　　　) costs and get it
   into mass production.
   コストを削減し大量生産するための研究が続いている。

2. Japan (　　　　　　　　　　　　　) imports for most of its coal needs.
   日本は、石炭需要のほとんどを輸入に依存している。

3. Tamio Ida (　　　　　　　　　　　　　) that technological innovation
   and soaring coal prices had brought the production cost of biocoke down to a
   decent level.
   井田民男氏は、技術革新と石炭価格の高騰によって、バイオコークスの製造コストは妥当な水準まで下
   がってきたと指摘した。

rely on	bring down	point out

Background Knowledge

CD 1-18

石炭の代替燃料を模索する企業の取り組みについて、英文に<u>述べられていないもの</u>を１～４から選びましょう。

　Japan relies on imports for most of its coal needs, with roughly 180 million tons of the stuff coming into the country in 2021, according to preliminary figures. About 10% of that was from Russia.

　An alternative fuel is even finding fans among major Japanese companies. Tokyo-based Mos Food Services Inc., which operates the Mos Burger fast food chain, began selling drinks made from coffee beans roasted with biocoke at 48 Mos Burger & Cafe stores in March. The raw material used for the solid fuel is used coffee grounds. A company representative explained, "As we considered renewing our coffee lineup, we were inclined to adopt environmentally friendly products. We would like to consider expanding our use of biocoke."

The Mainichi

1. 2021 年のデータによると、日本は約 1 億 8,000 万トンの石炭を輸入している。
2. 日本で利用されているバイオコークスの約 10% は、ロシアからの輸入に依存している。
3. 株式会社モスフードサービスは、バイオコークスで焙煎されたコーヒー豆から作られた飲料の販売を開始した。
4. 同社の担当者は、バイオコークスの利用拡大を検討したいと説明した。

Newspaper English

地名、人名や団体名など、「その人、ものだけにつけられた唯一の名前」のことを固有名詞といいます。固有名詞が複数語からなる場合は、語頭を大文字にして表記します。ただし、等位接続詞（and など）や前置詞は、大文字にせず小文字のままで表記されることが多いです。

以下の１と２の文には固有名詞が含まれています。固有名詞の箇所全てに下線を引きましょう。

1. The director of Bio-Coke Research Institute explained the production process of biocoke.

   バイオコークス研究所の所長が、バイオコークスの製造工程について説明した。

2. An alternative fuel to coal has been developed by Kindai University in Higashiosaka, Osaka Prefecture.

   石炭の代替燃料が、大阪府東大阪市にある近畿大学によって開発された。

Reading

Japanese firms look to plant-based, carbon-neutral "biocoke" fuel to cut CO$_2$ emissions

look to... 「〜に期待する」

Biocoke, a solid fuel made from vegetable waste materials, is attracting attention as one technology to help push the shift to a decarbonized society. Developed in 2005 by Kindai University in Higashiosaka, Osaka Prefecture, it is a "dream
5　solid fuel" that is said to emit virtually no carbon dioxide (CO$_2$) when burned.

solid fuel 「固形燃料」

virtually 「ほとんど」

Japan's restaurant sector and workshops in traditional industries are considering using biocoke as an alternative fuel, while research continues to bring down costs and get it
10　into mass production.

workshop 「作業場」

In April, Oitomi, a traditional Nambu ironware business in Oshu, Iwate Prefecture, tried replacing its usual coal coke with biocoke bricks made from apple lees and tree bark to melt cast iron. Oitomi senior managing director Akira
15　Kikuchi evaluated the iron kettle, wind chime, and paperweight produced in the experiment, and concluded, "There were more sparks than with coal coke alone, but there's no difference in quality."

replace A with B 「A を B に置き換える」

lees 「搾りかす」

tree bark 「樹皮」

cast iron 「鋳鉄」

Biocoke is made by shredding dried vegetable matter into
20　particles a few millimeters in size and compressing it under immense pressure. The material is then heated to about 180 degrees Celsius and formed into cylinders. The combustion temperature of biocoke is over 1,000 degrees Celsius, comparable to coal coke.

shred... 「〜を粉砕する」

particle 「粒子」

compress... 「〜を圧縮する」

combustion 「燃焼」

25　The biggest barrier to biocoke's success is the production cost. But Tamio Ida, director of Kindai University's Bio-Coke Research Institute, pointed out that "technological innovation and soaring coal prices have brought biocoke (production cost) down to a reasonable level."

soaring 「高騰する」

30　The most energy-consumptive part of the production process is the pretreatment of the raw materials, including drying and crushing them. According to Ida, costs can be reduced by selecting raw materials with low water content, such as buckwheat hulls and bran, and the outer skin of
35　wheat, and those that don't need grinding, like used coffee

buckwheat hulls 「そば殻」

bran 「ふすま」

grinding 「破砕」

grounds and tea leaves.

There are currently three companies producing biocoke. Since mass production is necessary to get it into general use, the institute is researching ways to improve the fuel's

40 performance, such as increasing its energy value and developing production technology. Ida commented, "We would also like to build a recycling-oriented supply chain, wherein local waste is converted into biocoke and consumed locally."

The Mainichi

Comprehension

本文の内容に合うように、1 と 3 の質問の答えとして適当なものを、2 の英文を完成させるのに適当なものを、a 〜 d から選びましょう。

1. What did Akira Kikuchi conclude after experimenting with the use of biocoke bricks?

   a. He found no distinct difference in product quality.

   b. The biocoke bricks produced an unreasonable amount of sparks.

   c. He believes it is necessary to experiment with alternative raw materials.

   d. Biocoke weighed less than the coal coke they ordinarily use.

2. According to Tamio Ida, biocoke production costs are at a reasonable level because

   a. used coffee grounds and tea leaves are readily available.

   b. the price of coal has dramatically increased.

   c. three companies have begun mass production of biocoke.

   d. of the increased availability of raw materials with low water content.

3. Which part of the biocoke production process consumes the most energy?

   a. Heating the raw materials to over 1,000 degrees Celsius.

   b. Converting recycled waste into biocoke.

   c. Drying and crushing the raw materials.

   d. Forming the biocoke into cylinders.

Summary

DL 12　CD1-20

以下の空所 1 〜 4 に当てはまる語を選択肢から選び、書き入れましょう。

Produced from organic waste materials, such as apple lees or buckwheat hulls, biocoke is a new type of carbon-neutral solid fuel that has shown (1.　　　　　　　　　　) in recent years. While production costs continue to present an (2.　　　　　　　　　　) to mass production, the Japanese restaurant sector and traditional workshops are considering its (3.　　　　　　　　　　) in their operations. Though further research is necessary to reduce costs and improve (4.　　　　　　　　　　), biocoke is nonetheless a promising technology as society moves toward a decarbonized future.

implementation　obstacle　potential　performance

Insights into Today's World

DL 13　CD 1-21

以下の対話の空所に、あなたのアイデアを書いてみましょう。その後、クラスメイトにその内容を伝えてみましょう。

Biocoke is recognized as one of the technologies that can promote a shift to a decarbonized society. **What else do you think can be done to move toward a decarbonized society?**

In my opinion, I think people should use _____

_____

Chapter 05

Dress Codes to Promote Gender Equality

よりよい労働環境を目指して

A woman working, dressed in a business suit of her own choice (The Asahi Shimbun)

Key Expressions 1

DL 14   CD 1-22

音声を聞いて 1 ～ 3 の（　　）内に適当な語を書き入れましょう。

1. A major department store in Osaka abolished uniforms for (e _ _ _ _ _ _ _ _) in 2003.

   大阪のある大手百貨店は、2003 年に従業員の制服を廃止した。

2. Female uniforms were introduced when the company was (f _ _ _ _ _ _) in 1952.

   その会社が 1952 年に設立された際、女性の制服が導入された。

3. The differences between male and female roles at banks have been gradually (e _ _ _ _ _ _ _ _ _).

   銀行における男女の役割の違いは、徐々になくなっている。

Key Expressions 2

1 〜 5 は企業の代表的な部署名です。日本語に当てはまる語を選択肢から選び、( ) 内に書き入れましょう。

1. 営業部 　　　(　　　　　　　　　　　　　　　)

2. 経理部 　　　(　　　　　　　　　　　　　　　)

3. 人事部 　　　(　　　　　　　　　　　　　　　)

4. 広報部 　　　(　　　　　　　　　　　　　　　)

5. 法務部 　　　(　　　　　　　　　　　　　　　)

> human resources department　　public relations department
>
> accounting department　　legal department　　sales department

Key Expressions 3

日本語訳を参考に、( ) 内に当てはまる〈助動詞 + have +過去分詞〉の表現を選択肢から選び、書き入れましょう。

1. Long-time customers of Kanako Katayama's teller window

(　　　　　　　　　　　　) something amiss.

片山加奈子さんの窓口の長年の顧客なら、何かおかしいと気づいたかもしれない。

2. The rule requiring female workers to wear uniforms (　　　　　　　　　　) much earlier.

女性だけが制服を着なければならないというルールは、もっと早く廃止されるべきだった。

3. It (　　　　　　　　　　) uncomfortable for women to wear high heels when they were not feeling well.

体調がよくないときにハイヒールの靴を履くのは、女性にとって不快であったに違いない。

> must have been　　should have been abolished　　might have noticed

● Background Knowledge

CD 1-23

埼玉大学の幅崎麻紀子准教授の述べる金融機関の窓口で女性が制服を着るようになった当時の事情について、英文に述べられているものを 1 〜 4 から選びましょう。

   Since the 1960s, during which Japan was experiencing rapid economic growth, banking institutions hired women in large numbers as tellers to promote their approachable image and attract new customers.

   The female-only uniform rule was established from the viewpoint of male executives who thought it would be difficult for female staffers to buy business suits when they were paid less than their male colleagues.   *The Asahi Shimbun*

Notes banking institution「金融機関」 teller「窓口係」 approachable「親しみやすい」

1. 1960 年代の銀行では、女性職員は普段着に近い親しみやすい服装が一般的だった。
2. 高度経済成長期、金融機関は多くの女性を男性と同じ待遇で雇った。
3. スーツを買うお金の余裕がなかった女性職員は、窓口係以外の仕事を担当した。
4. 女性のみ制服着用というルールは、男性職員より給与の低い女性職員に配慮して制定された。

● Newspaper English

「〜について、〜に関して」と言うとき、英文記事では 一般的でカジュアルな about よりも regarding や concerning が好まれます。このように形式的には -ing ですが前置詞のような働きをする語として、他にも including や considering があります。

日本語訳を参考に、1 と 2 の英文の（　　）内に入る語を選択肢から選び、書き入れましょう。なお、文頭に来る語も小文字で与えられています。

1. The provision (   ) the lending of uniforms was established in 1969.
   制服貸与に関する規定は、1969 年に制定された。

2. (   ) gender equality, the bank decided to abolish the female-only uniform.
   ジェンダーの平等を考慮して、その銀行は女性のみの制服を廃止することにした。

considering   including   regarding

Reading

Banks changing with the times by ditching female-only uniforms

Long-time customers of Kanako Katayama's teller window at the Kita-Urawa branch of Saitamaken Shinkin Bank in Saitama might have noticed something amiss.

Katayama, a regular employee, was dressed in a white
5 shirt, a black jacket and a pair of pants while some of the other female staff members were wearing uniforms.

Katayama said she can now choose any style of clothing she likes, in a change to the bank's dress code for women that dates back more than 50 years.

10 An increasing number of banking institutions are shedding a decades-old tradition of requiring only female workers to wear uniforms in a drive to promote gender equality.

One such example is the Shinkin Bank, which had
15 traditionally required female staff, except for those in managerial and sales positions, to wear a uniform consisting of a shirt available in pale blue and other colors, a vest, and a skirt or a pair of culottes.

But starting from May 2022, regular staff can wear a suit
20 or other business-appropriate attire. The same rule will be applied to part-time and temporary workers from May 2023.

According to a member of the human resources department, the rule to require only female workers to wear uniforms had apparently been in place for at least 50 years.

25 The provision regarding the lending of uniforms, which was established in 1969, states that uniforms are intended to maintain grace and elegance to improve work performance.

But when the company asked its staff through the employee union, some said they felt uncomfortable seeing
30 only female workers wearing uniforms, while others said they felt as if both insiders and outsiders of the company were seeing women in uniforms as subservient to men.

In fact, the majority were in favor of abolishing uniforms.

"We placed importance on eliminating the 'subservient
35 image' of women in uniform,"the member of the human

---

change with the times 「時代とともに変わる」

ditch... 「〜を捨てる、見捨てる」

regular employee 「正社員・正職員」

date back... years 「〜年前に遡る」

shed... 「(古い習慣など)を捨てる」

decades-old 「数十年来の」

in a drive to... 「〜させるために」

managerial and sales position 「管理職と営業職」

consist of... 「〜から成る」

business-appropriate attire 「仕事(職務)にふさわしい服装」

apply to... 「〜に適用する」

apparently 「どうも〜らしい」

be in place 「存続する」

grace 「品位、上品さ」

elegance 「気品、優雅さ」

improve work performance 「仕事の能率を上げる」

employee union 「従業員組合」

subservient 「補助的な」

in favor of... 「〜に賛成して」

place importance on... 「〜を重視する、〜に重点を置く」

resources department said. "We can gain the trust of our customers as we give them a favorable impression with the clothing we wear, instead of creating a unified appearance by wearing uniforms."

The Asahi Shimbun

gain trust「信頼を得る」
give... a favorable impression「〜に好感を与える」
unified「統一された、一元化された」
appearance「外見、見かけ」

Comprehension

本文の内容に合うように、1と3の英文を完成させるのに適当なものを、2の質問の答えとして適当なものを、a〜dから選びましょう。

1. According to the updated dress code at Saitamaken Shinkin Bank, female employees
   a. can now choose from a wide variety of uniforms.
   b. have the option of wearing a suit at work.
   c. do not need to follow any dress guidelines.
   d. should wear a skirt or a pair of culottes.

2. How long had the rule to require female workers to wear uniforms been in place?
   a. over 50 years
   b. from May 2023
   c. less than 50 years
   d. since the 1970s

3. The Saitamaken Shinkin Bank human resources department decided to update its dress policy
   a. because the previous policy presented an unfavorable image for customers.
   b. to promote the 'subservient image' of women in uniform.
   c. despite opposition from members of the employee union.
   d. in order to create a unified and elegant appearance.

● Summary

以下の空所 1 ～ 4 に当てはまる語句を選択肢から選び、書き入れましょう。

In an effort to promote gender equality in the workplace, banks in Japan are shifting their dress (1. _____) away from requiring female staff to wear uniforms. As these types of policies have been in place for (2. _____), some staff consider the tradition outdated and feel that it creates the appearance that the female staff members are inferior to their male (3. _____). To update the rules, some banks are offering female (4. _____) the option to wear the clothing of their choice.

employees   codes   colleagues   decades

● Insights into Today's World

以下の対話の空所に、あなたのアイデアを書いてみましょう。その後、クラスメイトにその内容を伝えてみましょう。

It is good to hear that banking institutions and department stores are eliminating uniforms for female employees. Japan, however, still ranked 125th out of 146 countries in the Global Gender Gap Report in 2023. **How can we improve gender equality in Japan?**

Well, as we all know, _____

_____

Chapter 06

Do You Dare Take the "Train to Apocalypse"?

ゾンビの手も借りたい

Zombies chase participants inside a train station in Jakarta (Kyodo)

● Key Expressions 1 　　　　🎧 DL 17 　◎ CD 1-27

音声を聞いて 1 ～ 3 の（　　）内に適当な語を書き入れましょう。

1. Zombies (c _ _ _ _) event participants inside a train station in Jakarta during a promotional campaign.

   ジャカルタの駅構内で、ある売り込みキャンペーン中にゾンビたちがイベント参加者を追いかける。

2. The event called "Train to Apocalypse" (e _ _ _ _ _ _ _ _ _) young people to use the new light rapid train.

   その「終末行き列車」と銘打たれたイベントは、若者に新型の軽量高速電車を利用するように促している。

3. PT Lintas Raya Terpadu Jakarta [PT LRT Jakarta] has been unable to (a _ _ _ _ _ _) many passengers because the route is too short.

   PT LRT ジャカルタ社は、同社の路線が短すぎるため、多くの乗客を集めることができないでいる。

Key Expressions 2

-er, -or という接尾辞は「〜する人」という意味を表す場合があります。1〜5の単語の下線部に適当な接尾辞を書き入れ、意味を選択肢から選び（　　）内に書き入れましょう。

1. operat _ _ 　　　　　（　　　　　　　　　　　　　　）
2. act _ _ 　　　　　　（　　　　　　　　　　　　　　）
3. organiz _ _ 　　　　（　　　　　　　　　　　　　　）
4. surviv _ _ 　　　　　（　　　　　　　　　　　　　　）
5. passeng _ _ 　　　　（　　　　　　　　　　　　　　）

乗客　　事業者　　俳優　　生存者　　主催者

Key Expressions 3

英文記事中で筆者が発話者の言葉や考えを伝えるのに、発言通りに伝える「直接話法」と、人称代名詞を変えるなどして筆者の言葉に変えて伝える「間接話法」という表現方法があります。1〜3はゾンビイベント体験者の発言についての英文です。話法に注意しながら空所に日本語訳を書き入れましょう。

1. "I wasn't expecting it to be this scary," a 15-year-old boy said during one event.
   15歳の男の子は、イベント中に「　　　　　　　　　　　　　　　　　　　」と話した。

2. A first-time LRT rider was pleased with the comforts of traveling by train, saying, "I'll take the train again on other occasions, but of course, not with the zombies on board."
   初めてLRT（軽量高架鉄道）に乗ったある乗客は、電車での移動の快適さに満足し、「　　　　　　　　　　　　　　　　　　　　　　　　　　　　　　　　　　　」と語った。

3. A horror movie enthusiast who joined her friends on the ride said they all had seen the movie but thought the event in Jakarta was even scarier, "probably because we experienced it ourselves."
   友人たちと一緒に乗車したホラー映画ファンの女性は、（　　　　　　　　　　　　　　　　　　　　　　　　　　　　　）、「おそらく　　　　　　　からです」と話した。

● Background Knowledge

CD 1-28

PT LRT ジャカルタ社の事務職員が 9 月に行われたイベントに関して語ったことについて、英文に述べられているものを 1 ～ 4 から選びましょう。

Sheila Maharshi, PT LRT Jakarta's corporate secretary, said the event, which ran through September, appears to have worked.

"This attraction has played a very significant role in increasing the number of LRT passengers, and we hope it can be a campaign to raise awareness of our service to attract more passengers in the future."

Kyodo News

1. 求職者に仕事を与えるという効果があった。

2. 乗客数の獲得には無関係であった。

3. 乗客数増加に大きな役割を果たした。

4. 車内サービスの向上に役立った。

● Newspaper English

英文記事では、読者の興味を引くために、しばしば事実と異なる状況を仮定して伝えることがあります。その場合、以下のような「仮定法」が用いられます。If 節を伴わない場合もあるので、助動詞の過去形が出てきたら、まず仮定法ではないかと考えるようにしましょう。

現在の事実と異なる状況を仮定する定型文（仮定法過去）

If 主語＋[動詞の過去形], 主語＋[助動詞の過去形＋動詞の原形].

1 と 2 は仮定法を含む英文です。日本語訳を参考に、下線部を適当な形に書き換えましょう。

1. If zombies be → _____ coming for you, what be → _____
_____ the best way to reach the safe zone?
　もしゾンビが襲ってきたら、安全地帯に行く最適の方法は何だろう。

2. The train operator suggest → _____ riding the metropolis's new light rapid train.
　もしその鉄道事業者なら、首都圏を走る新型の軽量高速電車に乗ることを提案するだろう。

Reading

 CD 1-29

Jakarta train firm holds 'zombie' event to scare up more passengers

JAKARTA — If zombies were coming for you in Jakarta, what would be the best way to reach the capital's "safe zone" — riding the metropolis's new light rapid train or driving through its notorious traffic?

5　The answer, the train operator would suggest, is the former — at least, that was the premise of a recent promotional campaign it staged for young people that saw them take 20-minute journeys while encountering disturbingly realistic zombies portrayed by actors at stops
10　along the way.

Encouraging young people to use public transportation was the objective of PT Lintas Raya Terpadu Jakarta and event organizer Pandora Box when launching the attraction in August, inspired by a popular South Korean horror movie.
15　It took place in station areas and inside the train cars.

Participants paid 60,000 rupiah (about $4), including the train fee of 5,000 rupiah, to join the fun. Called "survivors," the passengers were evacuated to another station that was declared to be the safe zone. Actors wearing military
20　uniforms and carrying toy rifles fought off the zombies while protecting the passengers and escorting them to safety.

The zombie actors were dressed in rags and wore makeup featuring eerily white eyes and blood-stained mouths. They dragged their feet along the tunnels and stairs and jumped
25　out suddenly at times.

Inside a train car with fake blood splattered on the walls, a television anchor announced that "the Pandora virus," originating in South Korea, had entered Indonesia, turning people into zombies within "3 minutes" of infection.
30　Called "Train to Apocalypse," the attraction was inspired by the 2016 South Korean thriller "Train to Busan."

Feby, a horror movie enthusiast who joined her friends on the ride, said they all had seen the movie but thought the event in Jakarta was even scarier, "probably because we
35　experienced it ourselves."

scare up... 「〜を怖がらせる」

notorious 「悪名高い」
the former 「前者」
premise 「前提」
stage... 「〜を行う」
encounter... 「〜に遭遇する」
disturbingly 「気味が悪いほど」
portray... 「〜を演じる」

objective 「目的」

inspired by... 「〜に着想を得て」

evacuate... 「〜を避難させる」
declare... 「〜と宣言する」
fight off... 「〜を撃退する」
escort... 「〜を案内する」
rag 「ぼろ服」
eerily 「不気味に、不自然に」
blood-stained 「血まみれの」
drag... 「〜をひきずる」
splatter... 「〜を飛び散らかす」

originate 「発生する」
infection 「感染」

Jakarta and its suburbs have a population of almost 33 million people, and traffic congestion and pollution are some of the capital's biggest headaches. LRT began commercial operations along a 5.8-kilometer stretch in December 2019 in
40 one of the efforts to improve the situation.

The service, however, has been unable to attract many passengers due to its short route, according to transportation experts. The route is expected to be expanded in the near future.   *Kyodo News*⁺

suburb「郊外」

traffic congestion「交通渋滞」

commercial operation「営業運転」

stretch「路線」

Comprehension

本文の内容に合うように、1 の質問の答えとして適当なものを、2 と 3 の英文を完成させるのに適当なものを、a ～ d から選びましょう。

1. Which of the following is true about the "Train to Apocalypse" promotion?
    a. It was inspired by a recent Indonesian horror film.
    b. Young people were the primary target audience.
    c. It failed to attract customers due to its short route.
    d. Some participants did not find it scary enough.

2. Passengers participating in the event
    a. were designated 'survivors' while traveling to their destination.
    b. wore costumes and realistic make-up to look like zombies.
    c. included actors portraying frightened bystanders.
    d. paid 65,000 rupiah to join.

3. The light rapid train was constructed in Jakarta
    a. to raise money to deal with the pollution problem.
    b. because there was no method of travel between the suburbs and the city center.
    c. in an effort to ease congestion on the city streets.
    d. to encourage elderly people to use public transportation.

● Summary

🎧 DL 18　　◎ CD 1-30

以下の空所 1 ～ 4 に当てはまる語を選択肢から選び、書き入れましょう。なお文頭にくる語も小文字で与えられています。

(1.) inspiration from the popular zombie horror film, "Train to Busan," the company that operates Jakarta's new light rapid train staged an elaborate promotional event on its trains and at its stations. The event saw participants (2.) for their lives as they used the train to travel to a safe zone, (3.) zombies along the way. With its limited route, the train has had trouble (4.) customers and event organizers aim to encourage city residents, particularly the young, to use public transportation more.

avoiding　　attracting　　running　　taking

● Insights into Today's World

🎧 DL 19　　◎ CD 1-31

以下の対話の空所に、あなたの意見を書いてみましょう。その後、クラスメイトにその内容を伝えてみましょう。

This zombie event by the train operator in Jakarta seems to have been an effective strategy for attracting more passengers. **What do you think about using such an event as a promotional campaign?**

I think _____

_____

Chapter

Chapter 07

Island Doctor Saves the Day

離島医療に向き合って

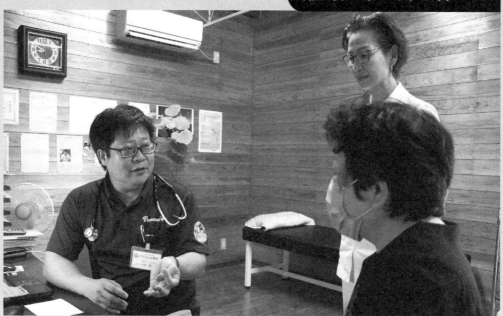

Shinsuke Kobayashi examines a patient in Yoron, Kagoshima Prefecture (The Japan News)

Key Expressions 1

🎧 DL 20   ◎ CD 1-32

音声を聞いて 1 ～ 3 の（　　）内に適当な語を書き入れましょう。

1. With (e _ _ _ _ _ _ _ _ _ _ _) from his grandmother, who was a pediatrician,
   Kobayashi pursued a career as a doctor.
   小児科医だった祖母の勧めで、小林さんは医師としての道を進んだ。

2. Kokawa always closely attended to his (p _ _ _ _ _ _ _), sometimes using the
   island's dialect.
   古川さんは、ときにはその島の方言を使い、いつも患者に寄り添って世話をした。

3. Kobayashi (t _ _ _ _ _) 20 to 30 people on most days.
   小林さんはほぼ毎日 20 ～ 30 人の人々を診療する。

Key Expressions 2

1 〜 5 はへき地医療の分野で話題に上る用語です。日本語に当てはまる語を選択肢から選び、（　　）内に書き入れましょう。

1. 遠隔医療　　　　　（　　　　　　　　　　　　　　　）
2. 在宅医療　　　　　（　　　　　　　　　　　　　　　）
3. 遠隔手術　　　　　（　　　　　　　　　　　　　　　）
4. 外科医　　　　　　（　　　　　　　　　　　　　　　）
5. 手術用ロボット　　（　　　　　　　　　　　　　　　）

> surgical robot　　remote medicine　　home health care　　surgeon　　telesurgery

Key Expressions 3

日本語訳を参考に、1 〜 3 の英文の［　　］内の語句を正しい語順に並べ替え、仮定法頻出の表現を完成させましょう。なお、文頭に来る語も小文字で与えられています。

1. If [for / not / had / been / it] the available home health care, I would have left the island.
   利用可能な在宅医療がなかったら、島を離れてしまっていただろうに。

   _____

2. [from / without / his grandmother / advice], Kobayashi might not have enrolled in Kagoshima University's Faculty of Medicine.
   祖母からのアドバイスがなければ、小林さんは鹿児島大学医学部に入学することはなかったかもしれなかっただろう。

   _____

3. [for / skill / but / the surgeon's], he would be dead now.
   その外科医の技術がなければ、彼は今ごろ亡くなっていただろう。

   _____

Background Knowledge

CD 1-33

日本における遠隔手術について、英文に述べられているものを1〜4から選びましょう。

Telesurgery, including the practice of surgeons in urban areas remotely performing surgery on patients in rural areas, is heading toward practical use in Japan.

Behind this is the advancement of telecommunications technology, which has made it safer to manipulate surgical robots from a distance. The innovative medical procedure is particularly promising for rural residents because it will allow advanced surgeries to be performed even in areas with few surgeons.

The Japan News

Notes telecommunications technology「電気通信技術」 manipulate...「〜を操作する」 medical procedure「医療（処置）」 promising「期待できる」

1. 遠隔手術ができる都市部の外科医が少ないため、遠隔手術の実現は困難である。
2. 電気通信技術の進歩が、離れた場所からの手術ロボットの操作をより安全にした。
3. 遠隔手術という革新的な医療は、特に都会に暮らす人々にとって期待できるものである。
4. 外科医のほとんどいない地域では、今後も先進的外科手術を行うことは不可能だろう。

Newspaper English

 英文記事では、場所や物などの位置を示す表現がよく用いられます。方角を示す表現にも慣れておきましょう。

日本語訳を参考に、1と2の英文の（　　）内に入る語を選択肢から選び、書き入れましょう。

1. Yoron Island is (　　　　　　　　　) about 560 kilometers south of Kagoshima City.

   与論島は、鹿児島市の南およそ 560 キロメートルに位置している。

2. The small clinic (　　　　　　　　　　) in the foothills of Mount Hakuba.

   その小さな診療所は、白馬山麓にある。

   lies　　located

Reading

Captivated by island, doctor relocates to treat residents

captivated by...「～に魅了されて」
relocate「移住する」
resident「住民」

A private clinic on a remote island 23 kilometers from the northern tip of Okinawa Island has finally reopened after it had to close for 16 months due to the lack of a doctor.

the northern tip of Okinawa Island「沖縄本島の最北端」
due to...「～のために」

Shinsuke Kobayashi moved from Tokyo and took over as
5 the clinic's director. The 42-year-old doctor said he wanted the clinic to help islanders feel at ease.

take over「引き継ぐ」
clinic's director「診療所の院長」
feel at ease「安心する」

The town of Yoron, Kagoshima Prefecture, consists only of Yoron Island. It is home to roughly 5,000 people and is located about 560 kilometers south of Kagoshima City.
10 Kobayashi's clinic is near the town hall.

consist of...「～から成る」
roughly「およそ」
town hall「町役場」

Kobayashi first visited Yoron Island during his university's remote medicine training program in his third year of school. He stayed on the island and learned under Seiji Kokawa, the previous director, for about 10 days.
15 Kobayashi was deeply impressed with how Kokawa, who opened the clinic in 1991, interacted with his patients.

training program「研修プログラム」
previous「前の」
be impressed with...「～に感銘を受ける」
interact with...「～と交流（対話）する」

After graduating from medical school at the age of 30, Kobayashi worked as a specialist in home health care at the Tokyo-based Yushoukai Medical Corporation.

Yushoukai Medical Corporation「医療法人社団　悠翔会」

20 Meanwhile, Kokawa, who was over 70, felt his physical strength reaching its limit and began searching for a successor to his clinic. Since he couldn't find one, Kokawa closed the clinic in March 2021. After consulting with the Yushoukai chairperson, whom Kokawa happened to know,
25 Kobayashi was singled out as a candidate.

physical strength「体力」
reach one's limit「～の限界に達する」
successor「後継者」
happen to...「たまたま～する」
single out...「選び出す」
candidate「候補者」

Kobayashi readily agreed, moving to the island from Tokyo in March 2022. In July, the clinic reopened under the management of Yushoukai.

readily「すぐに、快く」
under the management of...「～の運営の下」

Kobayashi treats 20 to 30 people on most days and
30 responds whenever he receives a call, even at night or on holidays. Many islanders wish to spend their last days at home, and there is a great demand for home health care, according to clinic staff. Kobayashi said he was once thanked by an islander, who told him that if it had not been for the
35 available home health care, he would have left the island.

a great demand for...「～に対する大きな需要がある」
islander「島民」

The clinic will begin accepting medical students from Kagoshima University for training in January 2023.

"I would be happy if the students who will come here for training would help us in the future," Kobayashi said,
40 recalling how he came to become the director.

The Japan News

recall... 「〜を思い出す」

come to... 「〜するようになる」

● Comprehension

本文の内容に合うように、1と2の英文を完成させるのに適当なものを、3の質問の答えとして適当なものを、a〜dから選びましょう。

1. Shinsuke Kobayashi

    a. briefly visited Yoron Island while in medical school.

    b. worked as a remote medicine specialist at Yushoukai Medical Corporation.

    c. graduated from medical school when he was 42 years old.

    d. reopened the clinic on Yoron Island in March of 2021.

2. Kobayashi greatly admired the way Seiji Kokawa

    a. managed the staff at the private clinic.

    b. pushed the limits of his physical strength.

    c. communicated with patients under his care.

    d. trained visiting medical students.

3. Which of the following is NOT true about the medical care Kobayashi provides to his patients?

    a. Support is provided for those wishing to die in the comfort of their home.

    b. Patients can expect to receive treatment outside of clinic hours.

    c. His clinic has set a limit of 30 patients per day.

    d. Home health care serves to make the island more livable for its residents.

● Summary

DL 21   CD 1-35

以下の空所 1 ～ 4 に当てはまる語を選択肢から選び、書き入れましょう。

When the opportunity arose, Shinsuke Kobayashi, a Tokyo-based physician, eagerly (^{1}.   ) the chance to relocate to Yoron Island in order to take charge of a private clinic that services the island's small population. This meant that the clinic could reopen, as it was (^{2}.   ) to close when the previous director (^{3}.   ) 16 months prior. The readily available medical care, particularly the home health care service that the clinic provides is greatly (^{4}.   ) by the island's residents.

retired   embraced   appreciated   forced

● Insights into Today's World

DL 22   CD 1-36

以下の対話の空所に、あなたのアイデアを書いてみましょう。その後、クラスメイトにその内容を伝えてみましょう。

The islanders must be delighted to have access to a doctor like Kobayashi. But I'm worried that he might overwork himself. **What can we do to help him?**

I see your point. _____

_____

Chapter 08

Changing Flavor with Magic

食器を変えるだけで減塩に

Ai Sato, developer of "Erekisoruto" (The Japan News)

Key Expressions 1

🎧 DL 23 ◎ CD 1-37

音声を聞いて1〜3の（　　）内に適当な語を書き入れましょう。

1. The salt intake of Japanese people (e _ _ _ _ _ _) the target value set by the Ministry of Health, Labor, and Welfare.

日本人の塩分摂取量は、厚生労働省が定める目標値を超えている。

2. The researcher focused on a technology that utilizes electrical power to (m _ _ _ _ _) a person's sense of taste.

研究者は、電力を利用して人の味覚を変化させる技術に着目した。

3. The "magic tableware" is (s _ _ _ _ _ _ _ _) to go on sale as early as the end of the year.

「魔法の食器」は、早ければ年末にも発売される予定だ。

Key Expressions 2

1〜5は本文に関連する健康科学分野にまつわる語句です。日本語訳を参考に、（　　）内に適当な語を選択肢より選び、書き入れましょう。

1. (　　　　　　　　) ions 　　　　　　［ナトリウムイオン］
2. (　　　　　　　　) flavored meals 　　［薄味の食事］
3. high (　　　　　　　) pressure 　　　　［高血圧］
4. (　　　　　　　　)-salt menus 　　　　［減塩メニュー］
5. (　　　　　　　　) therapy 　　　　　　［食事療法］

blood　　sodium　　reduced　　lightly　　dietary

Key Expressions 3

1〜3の（　　）内に適当な語を選択肢より選び、必要であれば形を変えて書き入れましょう。

1. At the time, Sato was (　　　　　　　　　　　) another research project.
   当時、佐藤氏は別の研究プロジェクトに取り組んでいた。

2. The researchers (　　　　　　　　　　) the latest technology called "electric taste."
   研究者たちは、「電気味覚」と呼ばれる最新技術に出合った。

3. The current prototypes (　　　　　　　　　　) two shapes: a bowl and a spoon.
   現在の試作品は、ボウルとスプーンの2つの形状で提供されている。

come across　　work on　　come in

Background Knowledge ⊙ CD 1-38

エレキソルトという技術の開発について、英文に<u>述べられていないもの</u>を 1 ～ 4 から選びましょう。

At the end of 2018, Ai Sato visited the laboratory of Professor Homei Miyashita at Meiji University. Miyashita is known as a leader in "electric taste" research, and after approaching him for cooperation, a full-scale joint research project began in 2019.

Not only does "Erekisoruto" enhance saltiness, but it also makes it easier to perceive umami and acidity as well. With the exception of foods with low water content, such as bread, "I think you will taste the difference in about 30 to 50% of meals you normally eat," Sato said.

The Mainichi

1. 宮下芳明教授は、「電気味覚」研究の第一人者として知られている。
2. 佐藤愛氏は、宮下教授と 2019 年に本格的な共同研究を開始した。
3. エレキソルトにより、塩味だけでなく、うま味や酸味も感じやすくなる。
4. 佐藤氏は「この技術によって、普段摂取している塩分量の約 30 ～ 50％をカットできる」と語った。

Newspaper English

英文記事では、会社名がよく登場します。英語表記の場合には、末尾に「会社」を意味する単語が正式名称ではなく略称で付くことが多く、その種類は様々です。同じ英語圏でも Ltd. は主にイギリスで使われ、Inc. は主にアメリカやカナダで使われるなど国による違いもあります。

以下の 1 ～ 4 は「会社」を意味する単語の略称です。正式名称のつづりに直して（　　）内に書き入れましょう。

1. Co.　　（　　　　　　　　　）
2. Ltd.　　（　　　　　　　　　）
3. Corp.　　（　　　　　　　　　）
4. Inc.　　（　　　　　　　　　）

Reading

What's cooking with Japanese developer's "magic tableware" that changes taste?

Ai Sato is a researcher at Kirin Holdings Co.'s health science division and the developer of "magic tableware." The development of this technology dates back to about five years ago. At the time, she was working on another research
5　project in collaboration with a university hospital, and heard doctors and nurses complain that even though they instructed their patients to reduce salt intake, it was hard to get them to continue eating lightly flavored meals.

The salt intake of Japanese people is high even by world
10　standards. The Ministry of Health, Labor and Welfare sets the daily intake target at less than 7.5 grams for adult men and 6.5 grams for adult women, but in reality, both men and women continue to exceed those targets by more than 2 grams.

15　Excessive salt intake can cause various diseases including high blood pressure. However, reduced-salt menus are somewhat tasteless. How can we cut the amount of salt while not sacrificing the "deliciousness" of the meal? While searching for a solution, Sato came across the latest
20　technology called "electric taste," which uses the power of electricity to change the way people perceive taste.

The outcome was "magic tableware." The current prototypes come in two shapes: a bowl and a spoon. Both allow the user to enjoy the electrically stimulated taste by
25　simply holding them, which naturally brings the user's hand into contact with the electrodes.

The products have been well received, and when 31 people undergoing salt reduction treatment tested them, 29 responded that they increased the salty taste. Kirin has
30　named the technology "Erekisoruto," a portmanteau of "electric" and "salt," and it is in the final stages of development for commercialization.

Sato has high expectations for the future of the technology. "In addition to health-related aspects like dietary therapy,
35　salt reduction is also a major challenge for the beauty and

division 「部門」
data back to... 「～にさかのぼる」

collaboration 「共同」
complain... 「～について不満を言う」
patient 「患者」

excessive 「過剰な」

sacrifice... 「～を犠牲にする」

perceive... 「～を知覚する」
outcome 「結果」

stimulated 「刺激された」

electrode 「電極」

undergo... 「～を受ける」
respond 「回答する」
portmanteau 「合成語」

commercialization 「商品化」
expectation 「期待」
aspect 「側面」

sports industries," she said. "I hope that Erekisoruto will become a catalyst for people to easily reduce their salt intake."

catalyst「きっかけ、触媒」

The Mainichi

● **Comprehension**

本文の内容に合うように、1の質問の答えとして適当なものを、2と3の英文を完成させるのに適当なものを、a～dから選びましょう。

1. Which of the following is true about the salt intake of Japanese people?

   a. It is higher than the targets set by the national government.

   b. The salt intake is low compared to other countries.

   c. Women tend not to exceed the target intake of 6.5 grams per day.

   d. The target daily intake is lower for men than it is for women.

2. Ai Sato

   a. worked as a researcher at a university hospital for five years.

   b. believes "erekisoruto" will appeal to a variety of industries.

   c. is the originator of "electric taste" technology.

   d. came up with the name "erekisoruto."

3. "Magic tableware" products

   a. use electricity to reduce the salt content of food.

   b. have performed poorly among test subjects.

   c. are activated by making contact with the user's hand.

   d. can be harmful for those undergoing salt reduction treatment.

Summary

DL 24 CD 1-40

以下の空所 1 〜 4 に当てはまる語を選択肢から選び、書き入れましょう。

To combat the health complications that come from diets that are (¹.   ) high in salt, researcher Ai Sato developed "magic tableware." Taking the current form of a bowl and spoon, these (².   ) ordinary household items (³.   ) alter the way people perceive the taste of food using a revolutionary technology dubbed, "erekisoruto." Sato's products have tested well and will soon become (⁴.   ) available.

seemingly   exceedingly   commercially   electrically

Insights into Today's World

DL 25 CD 1-41

以下の対話の空所に、あなたのコメントを書いてみましょう。その後、クラスメイトにその内容を伝えてみましょう。

Excessive salt intake is certainly unhealthy, so it's good to hear about the development of technology for reducing the amount of salt in our diets. **Are you doing anything to keep yourself healthy?**

I try to _____

_____

Chapter 09

Rethinking Our Relationship with Animals in Captivity

アニマルウェルフェアについて考える

Giraffes eat food from high-hanging baskets at Tama Zoological Park (The Yomiuri Shimbun)

Key Expressions 1

 DL 26　 CD 1-42

音声を聞いて 1 ～ 3 の（　　）内に適当な語を書き入れましょう。

1. Zoos and aquariums around Japan are reconsidering how they exhibit animals in their care and how visitors are allowed to (i _ _ _ _ _ _ _) with the animals.

日本国内の動物園や水族館は、飼育している動物をどのように展示するのか、またどのようにして訪問客に動物と触れ合ってもらえるのかを再検討している。

2. These efforts have been made to reduce stress on the (c _ _ _ _ _ _) creatures.

これらの取り組みは、閉じ込められた動物に対するストレスを緩和するためになされてきた。

3. The dolphin show that has been popular at an aquarium will be (d _ _ _ _ _ _ _ _ _ _) to coincide with the aquarium's renewal.

ある水族館で人気のイルカショーが、水族館のリニューアルに伴い取りやめになる予定である。

Key Expressions 2

1 ～ 6 は前置詞を伴う熟語です。日本語訳を参考に、（　　）内に適当な前置詞を選び、熟語を完成させましょう。同じ前置詞を複数回使ってもかまいません。

1. interact (　　　　　　　　　)... 　　　　[〜と触れ合う、〜と交流する]
2. stem (　　　　　　　　)... 　　　　　　　[〜から生まれる]
3. cram (　　　　　　　　)... 　　　　　　　[〜に詰め込む]
4. be accompanied (　　　　　　　　) ... 　[〜に伴われる]
5. call (　　　　　　　　)... 　　　　　　　[〜を求める]
6. prohibit ...(　　　　　　　　) ~ing 　　[…に〜することを禁じる]

by　　from　　with　　for　　into

Key Expressions 3

〈to ＋動詞〉で表される不定詞の前には、しばしば不定詞の主語を表す〈for ＋動作主〉が来る場合があります。日本語訳を参考に、1 ～ 3 の英文の [　　] 内の語句を並び替えましょう。

1. The concept of animal welfare emphasizes the need [in / to / for / their natural / animals / live] habitats.
   動物福祉の考えは、動物たちが自然の生息地で生きる必要性を強調している。

   _____

2. Zoos and aquariums have recently been creating more opportunities [with / visitors / interact / to / directly / for] animals, not only by observing them but also through experiences touching and feeding them.
   動物園と水族館は近年、動物の展示を見ることを通じてだけでなく、触ったり餌をやったりする体験を通じて、訪問客が直接動物と触れ合える機会を増やしてきた。

   _____

3. Kyoto City Zoo prohibited visitors from picking up guinea pigs. Instead, the zoo installed plastic tubes [to / the backs / visitors / for / stroke / the animals / of] .
   京都市動物園は、訪問客がテンジクネズミ（モルモット）を抱っこするのを禁止した。その代わり、動物園は訪問客が背中をなでられるようプラスチックのチューブを設置した。

   _____

Background Knowledge

⊙ CD 1-43

日本動物園水族館協会が定めた基準に従うため多摩動物公園が行っている取り組みについて、英文に<u>述べられていないもの</u>を1～4から選びましょう。

The Japanese Association of Zoos and Aquariums established standards for appropriate facilities for each animal in September 2020. Tama Zoological Park in Hino, Tokyo, which constructed new housing for three Asian elephants in August last year, has adopted the standards, creating an area five times larger than the previous one and separating the areas for females and males to suit the females' habit of forming groups with their offspring.

Gravel has been placed in the park's zebra enclosure so that their hooves can wear down naturally. The park also hangs giraffes' food baskets at a height that allows them to stretch their long necks and eat comfortably. *The Japan News*

Notes offspring「子」 hooves「ひづめ（hoof の複数形）」

1. 昨年8月に建てたアジアゾウのゾウ舎を取り壊した。
2. 基準に合わせて、以前のゾウ舎をかつてのものの5倍の大きさのものに建て替えた。
3. メスは子ゾウと一緒にグループを作りたがる習性があるため、メスとオスのエリアを分割した。
4. シマウマの囲い地には砂利を敷き、キリンには首を伸ばして楽に食べられるように、高所に食料かごを設置している。

Newspaper English

 英文記事の写真の下にはキャプションと呼ばれる説明文が付けられています。写真の中で誰が何をしているのかに加え、時や場所に関する情報も与えられることがあります。

a～cを並べ替え、以下の写真のキャプションを完成させましょう。

Giraffes eat food (　　　)(　　　)(　　　)

a. in Hino, Tokyo, on Aug 9

b. at Tama Zoological Park

c. from high-hanging baskets

Reading

Zoos move to reduce stress for animals in their care

Zoos and aquariums nationwide are reexamining how they exhibit animals in their care and how visitors are allowed to interact with the animals, so as to reduce stress on the captive creatures.

5   These efforts stem from the concept of animal welfare, which emphasizes the need for animals to live in their natural habitats.

In early August, when a dolphin jumped and splashed back into the water at an aquarium in the Kanto region, 10 families crammed into the auditorium during their summer vacation shouted with delight.

The dolphin show has been a popular feature since the aquarium's opening in 1991, but the aquarium decided to discontinue the show to coincide with its renewal of the 15 aquarium.

An animal protection group had sent in a petition accompanied by many signatures complaining that keeping the animals in the narrow, shallow pool for a show is abusive.

20   "There were many who regretted the decision to discontinue the show, but we took into consideration the concept of animal welfare," one of the staff said.

In June, Sapporo passed the nation's first municipal zoo ordinance following the death of a female sun bear that died 25 as a result of a fight with a male at the Maruyama Zoo, a popular zoo in the city.

The ordinance called for the creation of a breeding environment in which animals could live without stress or pain. As a general rule, it prohibits visitors from touching 30 the animals in the zoo's care.

Zoos and aquariums have recently been creating more opportunities for visitors to directly interact with animals, not only through observing animal exhibits but also through touching and feeding experiences.

35   However, the World Association of Zoos and Aquariums,

splash「水しぶきをあげる」

auditorium「観覧席」

petition「嘆願書」
signature「署名」

abusive「虐待的な」

municipal「市の」
sun bear「マレーグマ」

breeding environment「飼育環境」

the World Association of Zoos and Aquariums「世界動物園水族館協会」
headquartered in...「〜に本部のある」

headquartered in Switzerland, issued guidelines in 2015 that declared the necessity of ensuring animals' psychological well-being, given that animals may exhibit threatening behavior due to discomfort or stress.

40　　In light of the fact that insufficient efforts by zoos and aquariums in Japan could hinder the procurement of animals from overseas, the Japanese Association of Zoos and Aquariums also established standards for appropriate facilities for each animal in September 2020.

well-being「幸福」
discomfort「不快感」
in light of...「〜の点からみて」
hinder...「〜を妨げる」
procurement「調達」
establish...「〜を定める」

The Japan News

● Comprehension

本文の内容に合うように、1と2の英文を完成させるのに適当なものを、3の質問の答えとして適当なものを、a〜dから選びましょう。

1. The concept of 'animal welfare' places importance on

　a. the food animals consume when in captivity.

　b. the separation of captive creatures from humans.

　c. the ability of animals to breed naturally.

　d. the environment in which a captive animal lives.

2. An aquarium decided to discontinue the dolphin show

　a. following the death of an animal during a show.

　b. because visitors began to complain about the treatment of the animals.

　c. in response to efforts by animal rights activists.

　d. since the shows have been less popular in recent years.

3. Why did the Japanese Association of Zoos and Aquariums decide to establish standards for animal facilities in September 2020?

　a. Without such standards, it may become difficult to obtain animals from abroad.

　b. They were inspired by Sapporo's municipal zoo ordinance, which was the first in the country.

　c. In order to prohibit visitors from having physical contact with captive animals

　d. Because of the recent increase in stress levels among animals in captivity

Summary

DL 27　　CD 1-45

以下の空所 1 ～ 4 中に当てはまる語句を選択肢から選び、書き入れましょう。

> With the concept of animal welfare at the forefront, zoos and aquariums throughout Japan are taking (1.　　　　　　　　) to improve their (2.　　　　　　　　) and alter their practices in order to ensure animals' well-being. The cancellation of dolphin (3.　　　　　　　　) and the creation of stress-free breeding environments are among the changes taking place. Additionally, in an effort to stay in line with international (4.　　　　　　　　), nationwide standards for zoos and aquariums have recently been established.

shows　　facilities　　guidelines　　steps

Insights into Today's World

DL 28　　CD 1-46

以下の対話の空所に、あなたの考えを書いてみましょう。その後、クラスメイトにその内容を伝えてみましょう。

An animal protection group collected signatures and presented a petition complaining that it is abusive for the dolphins to be kept in a narrow, shallow pool for shows at an aquarium. **What do you think about that?**

Let me see. _____

_____

Chapter 10

Movie House Turned Club House

学校が苦手？ 映画館へいらっしゃい

Megumi Naoi, second from right, secretary-general of the nonprofit organization Aidao (Asahi)

Key Expressions 1

🎧 DL 29   💿 CD 1-47

音声を聞いて 1 〜 3 の（　　）内に適当な語を書き入れましょう。

1. Megumi Naoi, second from right in the picture, secretary-general of the nonprofit organization Aidao, speaks to a junior high schooler who is a (r _ _ _ _ _ _ _ _) member of the Ueda Kodomo Cinema Club at the Ueda Eigeki in Ueda, Nagano Prefecture.

   長野県上田市の上田映劇で、NPO 法人アイダオの直井恵事務局長（写真の右から 2 人目）が、「うえだ子どもシネマクラブ」の登録メンバーの中学生に話しかけている。

2. Free movies are shown (t _ _ _ _) a month at the cinema by three nonprofit organizations.

   NPO 法人 3 団体によって、無料の映画がその映画館で月 2 回上映されている。

3. The (a _ _ _ _ _ _ _ _) are designed for young people who are more apt to be isolated.

   その活動は、より孤立しがちな若い人たちを対象にしている。

Key Expressions 2

-ion は名詞をつくる接尾辞です。動詞につけると「〜の状態、〜であること、〜すること」などの意味合いを持つ名詞になります。語尾を変化させる必要のある動詞も多いため、注意しましょう。

例にならって、1〜6の動詞を名詞形にし、意味を選択肢から選び［　　　］内に書き入れましょう。

例）　act（action）［行動］

1. succeed　　　(　　　　　　　　　　　)［　　　　　　　　　]
2. interact　　　(　　　　　　　　　　　)［　　　　　　　　　]
3. isolate　　　(　　　　　　　　　　　)［　　　　　　　　　]
4. preserve　　　(　　　　　　　　　　　)［　　　　　　　　　]
5. utilize　　　(　　　　　　　　　　　)［　　　　　　　　　]
6. graduate　　　(　　　　　　　　　　　)［　　　　　　　　　]

卒業　　孤立　　活用　　交流　　連続　　保存

Key Expressions 3

日本語訳を参考に、1〜3の（　　　）内に当てはまる up を伴う熟語を選択肢から選び、書き入れましょう。

1. When the signboard of the Ueda Kodomo Cinema Club was placed in front of the century-old theater, children were seen (　　　　　　　　　　　) in succession to enter.

   その100年の歴史を持つ映画館前にうえだ子どもシネマクラブの看板が置かれたとき、子どもたちが次々と並んで、入場していく姿が見られた。

2. Of the 76 registered Cinema Club members, 21 children (　　　　　　　　　　　) that day, with 15 guardians and helpers (　　　　　　　　　　　) as well.

   シネマクラブ登録メンバー76名のうち、その日は21名の子どもたちがやってきて、15名の保護者や支援者たちも一緒に来ていた。

3. When children are (　　　　　　　　　　　) studying every day at school, they can go to the cinema and talk with others.

   子どもたちは、毎日学校で勉強することに飽き飽きしたときには、映画館に行き、他の人と話をすることができる。

showing up　　lining up　　fed up with　　turned up

Background Knowledge

 CD 1-48

上田映劇の上映会の様子について、英文に<u>述べられていないもの</u>を 1 ～ 4 から選びましょう。

Even as the film started, some children were still absorbed in painting in the cafe beside the lobby. Kids can choose how to spend their time, as the nonprofit groups' staff members will play with them in the cafe. Those tired of watching the movie can leave for another activity.

During the lunch break and following the afternoon showing, small children and other young people were playing a video game on a tablet computer or talking with adults in the lobby.

The Asahi Shimbun

Note be absorbed in... 「～に夢中になる」

1. 映画が始まっても、絵を描くのに夢中になっている子どもたちもいた。
2. 子どもたちは昼休みにタブレットコンピュータでゲームをしていた。
3. 映画を見飽きた子どもたちは別の活動をすることもできる。
4. 午後の上映終了後は、映画を見た人が感想を語り合うことになっている。

Newspaper English

 英文記事では、当該ニュースの起こった「時」やそのニュースに関連する事象が起こった「時」が動詞の時制で明確に伝えられますが、時を表す表現も伴う場合もあります。

日本語訳を参考に、1 ～ 3 の（　　）内に当てはまる語を選択肢から選び、書き入れましょう。

1. A film screening event is held on two occasions (　　　　　　　　　　) month at the theater.
   その映画館では、上映会が毎月 2 回開催される。
2. On a (　　　　　　　　　) summer day, the signboard of the Ueda Kodomo Cinema Club was placed in front of the century-old Ueda Eigeki theater shortly (　　　　　　　　　) 10 a.m.
   最近のある夏の日、朝 10 時少し前、100 年の歴史を持つ上田映劇前に「うえだ子どもシネマクラブ」の看板が置かれた。
3. The film will be shown the week (　　　　　　　　　) next in the theater.
   その映画は、その映画館で再来週上映される予定である。

recent	after	before	every

Reading

Old cinema opens doors to truant children, offering life lessons

truant「不登校の」

UEDA, Nagano Prefecture — On a recent summer day, the signboard of the Ueda Kodomo Cinema Club was placed in front of the century-old Ueda Eigeki Theater shortly before 10 a.m. Elementary and junior high school students
5 were seen popping up in succession to enter.

Volunteers here are providing truant children who find it difficult to go to school with an environment in which they can feel comfortable through encounters with a range of films and people at the theater.

provide... with ~「…に~を提供する / 与える」
encounter「出会い」

10 A free movie is offered twice a month at the Ueda Eigeki movie house by three nonprofit organizations. The activities cater to those from younger generations since they are more apt to be isolated.

cater to...「~を対象とする」

On Aug. 8, "Zannen na Ikimono Jiten the Movie" (the
15 movie version of "Encyclopedia of Pitiful Creatures") was shown in the morning. Children were given free popcorn in the lobby before taking their seats. Many came with their parents or siblings. Of the 76 registered Cinema Club members, 21 children turned up that day, with 15 guardians
20 and helpers showing up as well.

sibling「(男女区別しない) きょうだい」

Megumi Naoi, 43, secretary-general of the nonprofit organization Aidao, spoke to participants, saying "long time no see," "this is your first time, right?" and "have fun."

long time no see「久しぶりです」

The Cinema Club is run by Aidao and the Samurai
25 Gakuen Schola Imagine advocacy group, which helps youngsters live on their own, and an entity that shares the name of Ueda Eigeki to manage the screening, preservation and utilization of the theater. The joint program started two years ago with the goal of "taking advantage of a communal
30 cinema in an attempt to create a space to prevent isolation." The activity is funded through this fiscal year with a subsidy based on dormant deposits.

advocacy group「擁護団体」
live on one's own「一人暮らしをする」
entity「団体」
screening「上映」
in an attempt to...「~のために」
fiscal year「年度」
subsidy「助成金」
dormant deposit「休眠預金」

While the cinema screenings are usually held twice a month on Mondays, the office of another affiliated movie
35 house nearby is open every Wednesday and Friday to the

the office of another affiliated movie house「別館の事務所」

club's registered members.

Some visitors, including a junior high school student and a woman in her 20s who is struggling to become independent, come to the office to chat and study. They also engage in such

40 tasks as replacing posters.

Naoi said young people's involvement at the establishment is good for both the organizers and participants.

"I want those troubled by school affairs and post-graduation careers to learn something by sampling various

45 lifestyles and views via film," she said. "Coming to the cinema, visitors can converse with others. If they can also help out with trivial tasks, that is of great help to us."

The Asahi Shimbun

in one's 20s「20代の」

struggle to...「〜しようと奮闘する」

independent「自立（独立）している」

replace...「〜を取り換える」

involvement「参加、関与」

establishment「団体、施設」

career「進路、職業」

sample...「〜を手本にする」

converse with...「〜と会話する」

trivial task「雑用」

Comprehension

本文の内容に合うように、1と2の英文を完成させるのに適当なものを、3の質問の答えとして適当なものを、a〜dから選びましょう。

1. The activities offered at Ueda Eigeki cinema are designed for young people
   a. because students have a lot of free time after school.
   b. as they tend to be more interested in film than older generations.
   c. because they are more likely to be dealing with feelings of isolation.
   d. so that they can attract students and their siblings to the facility.

2. Registered Ueda Kodomo Cinema Club members
   a. are not allowed to attend screenings without a parent or guardian.
   b. pay a monthly fee that provides access to the theater and snacks.
   c. must be under 18 years old.
   d. can access the facility near the theater for a chat twice a week.

3. Which is NOT an activity that visitors to the Ueda Eigeki theater are likely to take part in?
   a. operating the film projector
   b. putting up a poster of the next film scheduled to be screened
   c. doing studying by themselves
   d. chatting with Cinema Club volunteers

Summary

🎧 DL 30   ⊙ CD 1-50

以下の空所 1 ～ 4 に当てはまる語を選択肢から選び、書き入れましょう。

> A group of nonprofit organizations cooperate to run the Ueda Kodomo Cinema Club at the 100-year-old Ueda Eigeki Theater in Ueda, Nagano Prefecture. The cinema serves as a (1.   ) where potentially isolated young people can experience community through meaningful (2.   ) with other members and club organizers, as well as participate in activities, including film screenings. Through a (3.   ) of activities, troubled young people can learn from (4.   ) to new perspectives.

range   space   interactions   exposure

Insights into Today's World

🎧 DL 31   ⊙ CD 1-51

以下の対話の空所に、あなたのアイデアを書いてみましょう。その後、クラスメイトにその内容を伝えてみましょう。

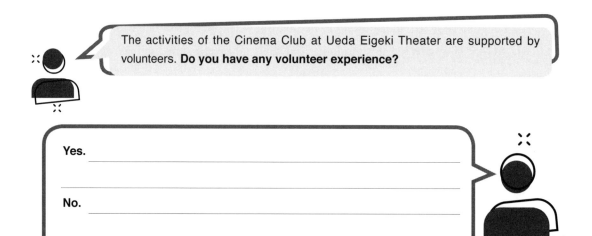

The activities of the Cinema Club at Ueda Eigeki Theater are supported by volunteers. **Do you have any volunteer experience?**

Yes. _____

_____

No. _____

_____

Chapter 11

Rice Is Out, Vegetables Are In

気候変動に応じた農業の在り方

A man removes weeds from a cabbage field in Manikganj, Bangladesh (Reuters/Aflo)

Key Expressions 1

DL 32   CD 2-02

音声を聞いて 1 ～ 3 の（　　）内に適当な語を書き入れましょう。

1. Climate change has made (r _ _ _ _ _ _ _) in Bangladesh unstable in recent years.
   近年、気候変動によりバングラデシュの降雨量が不安定になっている。

2. As groundwater began to dry up, the rice (h _ _ _ _ _ _) decreased.
   地下水が枯渇しだすと、米の収穫量が減少した。

3. Many farmers are switching from rice to vegetable (c _ _ _ _ _ _ _ _ _ _).
   多くの農家が、米から野菜の栽培へと切り替えている。

Key Expressions 2

> 語彙学習では、対照的な意味の語（反義語）もセットで覚えておくと、効率的に語彙を増やすことができます。

日本語訳を参考に、以下の1〜5の語について、与えられたアルファベットから始まる反義語を［　　］内に書き入れましょう。

1. erratic（不安定な）　⇔　[s　　　　　　　　　]（安定した）
2. production（生産）　⇔　[c　　　　　　　　　]（消費）
3. descendant（子孫）　⇔　[a　　　　　　　　　]（先祖）
4. supply（供給）　⇔　[d　　　　　　　　　]（需要）
5. send（送る）　⇔　[r　　　　　　　　　]（受け取る）

Key Expressions 3

日本語訳を参考に、1〜3の英文の（　　）内に適当な前置詞を選択肢から選び、書き入れましょう。

1. Cabbage has plenty of buyers and provides farmers (　　　　　　　　) a good income.
   キャベツには多くの買い手がいて、農家に良い収入をもたらす。

2. I didn't know what to do instead (　　　　　　　　) paddy farming.
   私は、水田農業の代わりに何をすべきか分からなかった。

3. Vegetable growing can produce higher yields and bring (　　　　　　　　) more money.
   野菜栽培は、より多くの収穫量を生み、より多くの金をもたらす可能性がある。

| of | with | on | in | at | as |

Background Knowledge ⊙ CD 2-03

バングラデシュの農業の現状について、英文に<u>述べられていないもの</u>を 1 〜 4 から選びましょう。

　While many farmers say their livelihoods have been saved by the discovery that vegetables can thrive on parched land, those abundant harvests can sometimes prove too much of a good thing.　In particularly productive seasons, oversupply drives down the prices farmers can charge for their produce, while storage is also an issue, said Hossain Ali, a farmer in the Godagari area of Rajshahi. When farmers grow more rice than they can sell, it can be dried and stored easily for six months, he said, but surplus vegetables quickly rot unless they are kept refrigerated.

Reuters

Note　parched「乾燥した」

1. 多くの農家は、野菜が乾いた土地で育つという発見によって生計が救われたと語っている。
2. 収穫量が豊富になればなるほど、生活の質が向上することが証明された。
3. ホセイン・アリ氏は、供給過多によって商品価格が低下したり、貯蔵も問題になると語った。
4. 農家が過剰に米を栽培しても、乾燥させれば 6 か月間は簡単に保存できる。

Newspaper English

 英文記事の中でおおよその数値情報を伝える表記方法として、「about」や「-odd」などがあります。

以下の 1 と 2 の英文では、おおよその数値情報が示されています。（　　　）内を埋めて、日本語訳を完成させましょう。

1. The farmer owns a cabbage farm of about 20 hectares.

その農家は、（　　　　　　　　　　　　　　）のキャベツ畑を（　　　　　　　　　　）。

2. He used to make 80,000-odd taka from his rice harvest.

彼はかつて（　　　　　　　　　　　　　）から（　　　　　　　　　　　　）を稼いでいた。

※ taka：タカ（バングラデシュの通貨単位）

Reading

Bangladesh farmers swap rice for vegetables as water dries up

For decades, Shafiqul Islam Babu, a 45-year-old farmer, grew rice on his land in northwest Bangladesh until climate change made rainfall more erratic, and overused groundwater began drying up in the mid-2000s. As his rice
5 harvest declined, so did his earnings.

erratic「不安定な」

earnings「収入」

In response, Babu decided to grow cabbage on his land — a high-value crop that uses less water than rice, has plenty of buyers and provides him with a steady income. "I didn't know what to do instead of paddy farming, which my family
10 has done for generations, and I had to maintain my family with my savings," he said in an interview while cleaning weeds and dead leaves from his 20-hectare cabbage farm. "Then, vegetable farming showed me a ray of hope."

high-value「高収益の」
crop「作物」

savings「貯金」

weed「雑草」
ray「光」

Babu said he sold his entire cabbage crop ahead of harvest
15 this year, with demand for the vegetable high in Dhaka, the capital. He managed to make about 215,000 taka ($2,000), up from the 80,000-odd taka he used to receive for his rice harvest.

capital「首都」

The accelerating impact of climate change has led many
20 farmers in Bangladesh's Rajshahi district to swap rice for vegetables as they strive to make their business pay on an ever-hotter planet. Eight years ago, rice was the region's main crop, but now it is the "loser crop," with vegetables from cabbage to gourds increasingly favored as they need
25 less water, produce higher yields and bring in more money, according to Shamsul Wadud, head of the district's Department of Agricultural Extension.

accelerating「加速する」
district「地区」
strive to...「～しようと努力する」

loser「敗者」
gourd「ウリ類」
favor...「～を好む」

Farmers in Rajshahi used to struggle to grow rice for two seasons a year, but many are now cultivating vegetables
30 three or four times annually on the same land, Wadud explained. "They are getting good prices and the production of vegetable crops has now increased many times," he said.

cultivate...「～を栽培する」
annually「1 年に」

Since 2009, the area of land dedicated to growing vegetables has almost quadrupled to about 78,500 hectares
35 in Rajshahi, making it the nation's largest vegetable-

dedicated to...「～に専用の」
quadruple「4 倍になる」

producing district, agriculture ministry figures show. But it's not just Rajshahi that is looking beyond rice. Bangladesh's Minister of Agriculture Muhammad Abdur Razzaque said the government was aiming to use "all kinds of abandoned
40 and sandy land" to expand vegetable production.

Reuters

ministry「省」
minister「大臣」
aim to...「〜を目指す」
abandoned「放棄された」
sandy「砂の」

Comprehension

本文の内容に合うように、1と2の英文を完成させるのに適当なものを、3の英文の空所に入るものとして適当なものを、a〜dから選びましょう。

1. Shafiqul Islam Babu's rice harvest declined because
    a. there was insufficient water to support his crops.
    b. the demand for rice decreased in the 2000s.
    c. his ancestors overused the groundwater on their land.
    d paddy farming is not a profitable profession.

2. In Bangladesh's Rajshahi district,
    a. rice has been considered a "loser crop" for the past eight years.
    b. it is impossible for farmers to harvest vegetables twice a year.
    c. growing vegetables is more profitable than growing rice.
    d. vegetable production has nearly quadrupled since 2009.

3. The government of Bangladesh would like to _____ vegetable production in the country.
    a. abandon
    b. curtail
    c. broaden
    d. halt

Summary

DL 33　CD 2-05

以下の空所 1 〜 4 に当てはまる語句を選択肢から選び、書き入れましょう。

In response to (¹·   ) harvests due to the impact of climate change, many farmers in the Rajshahi district in northwest Bangladesh are (²·   ) vegetables in place of rice, making it the nation's primary vegetable-producing district. This is largely because vegetables require less water than rice and the demand is higher, (³·   ) to increased profits for farmers. Additionally, the national government is (⁴·   ) plans to bolster vegetable production throughout the country.

leading   growing   declining   commencing

Insights into Today's World

DL 34　CD 2-06

以下の対話の空所に、あなたのアイデアを書いてみましょう。その後、クラスメイトにその内容を伝えてみましょう。

Bangladesh is experiencing erratic rainfall due to climate change. **What other impact is climate change having on our lives?**

Climate change is causing _____

_____

Chapter 12

Finding a Home Away from Home

住む国を選ぶ時代

Kyoko Tsukigase (right) has lived in Seattle since 2020 (Provided by Kyoko Tsukigase)

Key Expressions 1

DL 35　　CD 2-07

音声を聞いて1〜3の（　　）内に適当な語を書き入れましょう。

1. More and more Japanese nationals have chosen to live as (p _ _ _ _ _ _ _ _) residents abroad.

   ますます多くの日本人が、永住者として海外に住むことを選んでいる。

2. The number of Japanese residents overseas has been (s _ _ _ _ _ _ _) increasing in the past two decades.

   この20年で、海外に居住する日本人の数は着実に増えている。

3. Some may be (s _ _ _ _ _ _) a better environment for child-rearing or job opportunities.

   中には子育てのためのより良い環境や仕事の機会を求めていると思われる人もいる。

Key Expressions 2

動詞に様々な接尾辞を付けて名詞が作られます。-ent, -ant は「～をする人（もの）」、-ment は「結果・状態など」、-tion は「状態、（動作の）結果」という意味を持ちます。

上記の説明と日本語訳を参考に、1 ～ 6 の動詞を名詞にして [ ] 内に書き入れましょう。

1. reside（住む、居住する）　　　　　　[　　　　　　　　] （居住者）
2. immigrate（移住する）　　　　　　　[　　　　　　　　] （移住者、移民）
3. fulfill（満たす、充足する）　　　　　[　　　　　　　　] （充足）
4. appreciate（感謝する、ありがたく思う）[　　　　　　　　] （感謝）
5. communicate（伝達する）　　　　　　[　　　　　　　　] （伝達、通信）
6. describe（述べる、描写する）　　　　[　　　　　　　　] （記述、描写）

Key Expressions 3

日本語訳を参考に、1 ～ 3 の英文の（　　）内に適当な動詞を選択肢から選び、必要ならば形を変えて書き入れましょう。

1. A Tokyo man says he has never felt the desire to return to Japan, partly because of the effort he is (　　　　　　　　　　) in to learn the native language.
   ある東京の男性は日本に戻りたいと思ったことはないと述べる。現地の言葉を覚えるために費やしている努力もその一因である。

2. There are multiple reasons why women (　　　　　　　　　) up more than 60% of Japanese permanent residents abroad.
   日本人の海外永住者の 60% 以上を女性が占めている理由は複数ある。

3. Women (　　　　　　　　　) to be more open to experiencing a life overseas, but Japan's gender gap and the pursuit of work-life balance are also behind their choices.
   女性は海外の生活を経験することを（男性より）受け入れやすい傾向にあるが、日本のジェンダー差やワークライフバランス（仕事と生活の調和）を求めているということも彼女たちの選択の背後にある。

> make　　tend　　put

Background Knowledge

CD 2-08

外務省による 2022 年 10 月時点での海外在留邦人数調査統計について、英文に<u>述べられ</u><u>ていないもの</u>を 1 ～ 4 から選びましょう。

About half of Japanese nationals were permanent residents in North America, followed by Western Europe (16.2%), Oceania (13.7%), South America (11.7%) and the rest of Asia (7.7%). By country, the U.S. topped the list with about 220,000 permanent residents, followed by Australia and Canada. China ranked a distant second in the overall number of Japanese nationals living abroad (102,066) after the U.S. (418,842), but most were long-term residents and only 4,140 were permanent residents.

The Japan Times

1. 海外在留邦人の約半数が北米永住者で、次いで西ヨーロッパの永住者だった。
2. 邦人永住者数の国別の第 2 位は、オーストラリアであった。
3. 邦人の海外在留者の総数で 2 番目に多いのは、中国であった。
4. 中国にいる邦人長期滞在者は、たったの 4,140 人であった。

Newspaper English

 英文記事には、しばしば公的機関の調査結果や統計などの情報が盛り込まれます。いつのデータと比較されていて、どれくらい増えた／減ったかなどを知るために、英文で数字に関する情報を読む際には動詞、副詞、前置詞などに注目する必要があります。

1 と 2 の英文の（　　）に入る適当な語を選び、必要であれば形を変えて書き入れましょう。

1. In the survey released in December, 557,034 Japanese nationals were permanent residents overseas, with the figure steadily increasing in the past two decades and nearly (　　　　　　　　　　　　　　) from 285,705 in 2002.
   12 月に発表されたその調査では、55 万 7,034 人の日本人が海外の永住者となっており、その数は、過去 20 年で着実に増えており、2002 年の 28 万 5,705 人からおよそ 2 倍となった。

2. In total, the number of Japanese nationals living abroad — both long-term residents and permanent residents — was about 1.3 million, (　　　　　　　　　　　) 2.7% from the previous year.
   合計で、海外在留邦人の数は、長期滞在者と永住者を合わせて、前年から 2.7％減って約 130 万人であった。

down　　double

● Reading

 CD 2-09

A record number of Japanese nationals are now living as permanent residents abroad

A record number of Japanese nationals were living as permanent residents abroad in 2022 despite a decline in the overall number of people residing overseas, a recent Foreign Ministry survey showed.

5 In the survey released in December, 557,034 Japanese nationals were permanent residents overseas, with the figure steadily increasing in the past two decades and nearly doubling from 285,705 in 2002.

But the total number of long-term residents declined 6.9%
10 from the year before to 751,481, as many Japanese living abroad returned to Japan amid the COVID-19 pandemic, according to the survey. In total, the number of Japanese nationals living abroad — both long-term residents and permanent residents — was about 1.3 million, down 2.7%
15 from the previous year.

There could be a number of factors behind the steady rise of permanent residents abroad — from international marriages to people who decide to stay after being posted for work. Others may be seeking a better environment for child-
20 rearing or job opportunities.

Such is the case for Toshiki Tanaka, a 64-year-old pastor who has been living in Reykjavik, Iceland, since 1992 after marrying an Icelandic woman. The couple moved to Reykjavik after living in Nagoya for two years.

25 Born in Hachioji in western Tokyo, Tanaka has never felt the desire to return to Japan, partly because of the effort he is putting in to learning the native language, but also because he is fulfilled by his role as a pastor who works for immigrants and their families. He has also come to
30 appreciate the way people in Iceland are more open-minded.

"Europeans feel more comfortable asking for and giving others help, but Asians feel too embarrassed to open up about their worries," he said.

The Foreign Ministry survey also showed that of the
35 nearly 560,000 Japanese nationals living abroad as

record 「記録的な」

overall 「全体の、総〜」

factor 「要因」

post... 「〜を配属する」

Reykjavik 「レイキャヴィーク（アイスランドの首都）」

pastor 「牧師」

embarrassed 「恥ずかしがって」

open up... 「〜をおおっぴらにする、開示する」

permanent residents, about 62% were women.

Kyoko Tsukigase, 41, is one of them. The Tokyo native married a US national in 2017, got her green card in the summer of 2020 and moved to the United States that same year.

Tsukigase felt that there was a better work-life balance in America and the more direct communication style suited her better. She also thought Japanese society placed too much of a burden on women to perform child-rearing duties, which she described as "unfriendly" to women.

"There's not enough societal support," she said. "I say this not just from an economic perspective, but also from a cultural mindset. ... It's like the family unit comes second to society as a whole."

The Japan Times

green card「グリーンカード(外国人国内労働許可証)」

burden「負担」

perspective「観点」
mindset「考え方」
unit「単位」
as a whole「全体として」

● Comprehension

本文の内容に合うように、1 と 3 の英文を完成させるのに適当なものを、2 の質問の答えとして適当なものを、a 〜 d から選びましょう。

1. The number of Japanese nationals living abroad as permanent residents
   a. decreased by 2.7% from 2021 to 2022.
   b. nearly doubled over a period of 20 years.
   c. declined 6.9% as a result of COVID-19.
   d. stood at 285,705 as of December 2022.

2. Which is NOT one of the reasons why Toshiki Tanaka is content to stay in Iceland?
   a. He appreciates that the Icelandic people are more open to immigrants.
   b. He enjoys a high level of job satisfaction as a pastor.
   c. He respects the tendency of European people not to hide their concerns.
   d. He has worked hard to learn the Icelandic language.

3. Kyoko Tsukigase prefers life in the U.S. to life in Japan partly because
   a. women are more suited to the direct communication style of Western cultures.
   b. Japanese society places too much pressure on children.
   c. people are more friendly to women outside of Japan.
   d. it is easier to achieve a healthy work-life balance.

Summary

🎧 DL 36　◎ CD 2-10

以下の空所1～4に当てはまる語句を選択肢から選び、書き入れましょう。

While the number of Japanese nationals (1.   ) abroad decreased in 2022 amid the COVID-19 pandemic, the number of permanent residents overseas is consistently (2.   ) over the long term. This is due to a variety of factors, (3.   ) international marriages, employment opportunities, general cultural preferences, and child-rearing environments. A majority of this population consists of women, some of whom have chosen to escape the burden placed on Japanese women when it comes to (4.   ) children.

increasing　　living　　including　　raising

Insights into Today's World

🎧 DL 37　◎ CD 2-11

以下の対話の空所に、あなたのアイデアを書いてみましょう。その後、クラスメイト
にその内容を伝えてみましょう。

Did you know that more and more Japanese people have been leaving Japan to live in other countries recently? Living in a different country would be a big challenge for me! But I want to live overseas someday. **Which country would you like to live in if you had the chance? And why?**

I would choose _____

_____

Lessons Learned from a Chatbot

「会話型 AI」のお手並み拝見

Businessman using chatbot on smartphone (© Kiattisak Lamchan | Dreamstime.com)

● Key Expressions 1

🎧 DL 38　◎ CD 2-12

音声を聞いて 1 ～ 3 の（　　）内に適当な語を書き入れましょう。

1. OpenAI, one of the world's most ambitious AI research and deployment companies, (r _ _ _ _ _ _ _) an online chatbot called ChatGPT.

   世界で最も野心的な人工知能研究開発企業の 1 つである OpenAI 社は、ChatGPT というオンライン
   チャットボットを発表した。

2. Chatbots like ChatGPT can deliver facts, while also generating business plans, term paper topics and other new ideas from (s _ _ _ _ _ _).

   ChatGPT のようなチャットボットは、事実を伝えるだけでなく、ビジネスプランや学期末レポートの
   テーマなど、また別の新しいアイデアをゼロから生み出すことができる。

3. Companies such as Google and OpenAI can push chatbot technology forward at a faster rate than others, but they cannot (p _ _ _ _ _ _) people from using these systems to spread misinformation.

   Google 社や OpenAI 社などの企業は、チャットボットの技術を他社よりも速いスピードで推し進めることがで
   きるが、これらのシステムを利用して、人々が誤った情報を拡散することを阻止することはできない。

Key Expressions 2

-al、-ous は形容詞をつくる接尾辞です。例にならって 1 ～ 7 の下線部に適当な接尾辞を書き入れ、形容詞の意味を選択肢から選び [　　] 内に書き入れましょう。

例）fictional, fictitious [架空の]

1. technologic____　　　　　[　　　　　　　　　　　]
2. digit____　　　　　　　　[　　　　　　　　　　　]
3. artifici____　　　　　　　[　　　　　　　　　　　]
4. ambiti____　　　　　　　[　　　　　　　　　　　]
5. experiment____　　　　　[　　　　　　　　　　　]
6. person____　　　　　　　[　　　　　　　　　　　]
7. obvi____　　　　　　　　[　　　　　　　　　　　]

技術の　　個人的な　　人工の　　デジタルの　　野心的な　　実験用の　　明らかな

Key Expressions 3

疑問詞から始まり「?」で終わる直接疑問文と異なり、疑問詞から始まる名詞節が文の一部に組み込まれている場合、これを間接疑問文と呼びます。疑問詞の後ろは主語＋動詞の語順となり、動詞は主節の動詞と時制を一致させます。以下の 1 ～ 3 の直接疑問文を間接疑問文に変更し、下線部に書き入れましょう。

1. What is trigonometry good for?
   三角法はなんのためにあるのか。
   → She asked ChatGPT _____.
   彼女は三角法は何の役に立つのかを ChatGPT に尋ねた。

2. Where do black holes come from?
   ブラックホールはどこで生まれるのか。
   → Using the chatbot, she wanted to find out _____.
   彼女は、そのチャットボットを使って、ブラックホールはどこで生まれるのかを知りたかった。

3. Why do chickens incubate their eggs?
   なぜニワトリは卵をかえすのか。
   → The chatbot told her _____.
   そのチャットボットは、なぜニワトリは卵をかえすのかを彼女に教えた。

● Background Knowledge

CD 2-13

先進的なチャットボットについて、英文に述べられているものを 1 ～ 4 から選びましょう。

　OpenAI is among the many companies, academic labs and independent researchers working to build more advanced chatbots. These systems cannot exactly chat like a human, but they often seem to. They can also retrieve and repackage information with a speed that humans never could. They can be thought of as digital assistants — like Siri or Alexa — that are better at understanding what you are looking for and giving it to you.

The New York Times

1. 人間と全く同様にチャットすることができる。
2. 人間が決して追いつけないような速さで情報を処理する。
3. 取得した情報を変更したり、修正して再発信することはできない。
4. ユーザーが求めているものを提供するのは不得意である。

● Newspaper English

記事の中で紹介されている人物や事象が、唯一のものではなく複数ある中の一例であるということを示す表現に「one of the ＋ 複数名詞」があります。

日本語訳を参考に、（　　）内の語句を並べ替え、英文を完成させましょう。

Aaron Levie is CEO of a Silicon Valley company, Box, and (the technological landscape / will change / the ways / the many executives / these chatbots / one of / exploring).

アーロン・レヴィ氏は、シリコンバレーの企業、Box の CEO で、これらのチャットボットが技術的な展望をどう変えるかを探っている、多くの経営者の一人である。

Aaron Levie is CEO of a Silicon Valley company, Box, and ＿＿＿＿＿＿＿＿＿＿＿

＿＿＿＿＿＿＿＿＿＿＿＿＿＿＿＿＿＿＿＿＿＿＿＿＿＿＿＿＿＿＿＿＿＿＿＿＿＿＿

＿＿＿＿＿＿＿＿＿＿＿＿＿＿＿＿＿＿＿＿＿＿＿＿＿＿＿＿＿＿＿＿＿＿＿＿＿＿.

Reading

CD 2-14

The new chatbots could change the world. Can you trust them?

This month, Jeremy Howard, an artificial intelligence researcher, introduced an online chatbot called ChatGPT to his 7-year-old daughter. It had been released a few days earlier by OpenAI, one of the world's most ambitious AI labs.

5　He told her to ask the experimental chatbot whatever came to mind. She asked what trigonometry was good for, where black holes came from and why chickens incubated their eggs. Each time, it answered in clear, well-punctuated prose. When she asked for a computer program that could
10　predict the path of a ball thrown through the air, it gave her that, too.

Over the next few days, Howard — a data scientist and professor whose work inspired the creation of ChatGPT and similar technologies — came to see the chatbot as a new kind
15　of personal tutor. It could teach his daughter math, science and English, not to mention a few other important lessons. Chief among them: Do not believe everything you are told.

"It is a thrill to see her learn like this," he said. "But I also told her, 'Don't trust everything it gives you. It can make
20　mistakes.'"

After the release of ChatGPT — which has been used by more than 1 million people — many experts believe these new chatbots are poised to reinvent or even replace internet search engines such as Google and Bing.
25　"You now have a computer that can answer any question in a way that makes sense to a human," said Aaron Levie, CEO of a Silicon Valley company, Box, and one of the many executives exploring the ways these chatbots will change the technological landscape. "It can extrapolate and take ideas
30　from different contexts and merge them together."

The new chatbots do this with what seems like complete confidence. But they do not always tell the truth. Sometimes, they even fail at simple arithmetic. They blend fact with fiction. And as they continue to improve, people could use
35　them to generate and spread untruths.

come to mind「（アイデアなどが）心に浮かぶ」

well-punctuated prose「きちんと区切られた文体」

predict...「～を予測する」

path「軌道」

inspire...「～の着想を与える」

creation「創作」

not to mention「～は言うまでもなく」

lesson「教訓」

chief「重要な、主な」

thrill「ぞくぞくする感じを与えるもの」

poised「準備ができている」

reinvent...「～を改革する、新たに作り変える」

replace...「～に取って代わる」

make sense to...「～が理解できる」

extrapolate...「～を推定する」

context「文脈」

merge...「～を融合させる」

confidence「自信」

not always...「いつも～だとは限らない」

arithmetic「算数」

blend... with~「…を～と混ぜ合わせる」

Just as Howard hoped that his daughter would learn not to trust everything she read on the internet, he hoped society would learn the same lesson.

40 "You could program millions of these bots to appear like humans, having conversations designed to convince people of a particular point of view," he said. "I have warned about this for years. Now it is obvious that this is just waiting to happen."

The New York Times

designed to... 「～するように仕向ける」

convince... of～ 「…に～を納得させる」

point of view 「見解」

● **Comprehension**

本文の内容に合うように、1の英文を完成させるのに適当なものを、2と3の質問の答えとして適当なものを、a～dから選びましょう。

1. Jeremy Howard

　a. encourages skepticism when it comes to information shared by chatbots.

　b. was the chief designer and programmer of the ChatGPT project.

　c. always believes the responses to questions provided by ChatGPT.

　d. places strict limits on his daughter's use of chatbot technology.

2. What is one of the stated weaknesses of the latest chatbots?

　a. The computer programs they design tend to fail.

　b. They are not as accurate as existing internet search engines.

　c. They sometimes convey a mixture of fact and fiction.

　d. Their answers tend to have punctuation errors.

3. Which best describes Jeremy Howard's attitude toward the future use of chatbots?

　a. concerned

　b. comfortable

　c. confident

　d. optimistic

Summary

🎧 DL 39　◎ CD 2-15

以下の空所 1 〜 4 に当てはまる語を選択肢から選び、書き入れましょう。

With a wide range of abilities and a (1.　　　　　　　　　　)
bottomless well of knowledge to pull from, the latest chatbots are set to
(2.　　　　　　　　　　) alter the technological landscape by
assisting people with a variety of tasks and giving them instant access to
the information they seek. However, chatbots are also capable of
(3.　　　　　　　　　　) answering questions and making mistakes
when it comes to even the simplest of tasks. Additionally, experts warn of
the danger that they will almost (4.　　　　　　　　　　) be
used to manipulate users and shape their opinions.

falsely　　seemingly　　certainly　　substantially

Insights into Today's World

🎧 DL 40　◎ CD 2-16

以下の対話の空所に、あなたの質問を書いてみましょう。その後、クラスメイトにその内容を伝えてみましょう。

One time when I was playing around and asked an advanced chatbot to tell me a lie, it replied that it couldn't because its mission is to provide useful and truthful information. **What question would you like to ask a chatbot?**

I would ask it _____

_____

Food Opens a Gateway to Cultural Diversity

「食の多様性」を知る

Halal bread products prepared at the student cafeteria of the University of Miyazaki (Asahi)

● Key Expressions 1

🎧 DL 41　◎ CD 2-17

音声を聞いて 1 ～ 3 の（　）内に適当な語を書き入れましょう。

1. Halal bread products are (p _ _ _ _ _ _ _) at the student cafeteria of the University of Miyazaki.

   宮崎大学の学生食堂では、ハラールのパン製品が用意されている。

2. Halal foods do not contain any (c _ _ _ _ _ _ _ _) that are prohibited by Muslim scripture.

   ハラールフードは、イスラム教の経典（コーラン）で禁じられている成分を含んでいない。

3. Under Islamic law, eating is like praying, so (c _ _ _ _ _ _ _) halal foods is very important for Muslims.

   イスラム法の下では、食事は祈りと同じであり、イスラム教徒にとってハラールフードを摂取することは非常に重要なことである。

Key Expressions 2

長文読解において未知の単語に出合ったときに、知っている単語の派生語であるかどうかに気づく力は重要です。もし派生語なら、品詞や文脈を手掛かりに意味を推測することができるからです。

例にならって、1〜6の単語の意味を参考に、まず各派生語の品詞を［　　］内に書き入れ、品詞に合わせた意味を（　　）内に書き入れましょう。

例）pay（支払う）―― payment ［名詞］（支払い）

1. produce...（〜を製造する）―― product 　　［　　　　　］（　　　　　　　　　　）
2. offer...（〜を提供する）　　―― offering 　　［　　　　　］（　　　　　　　　　　）
3. certify...（〜を認証する）　―― certification ［　　　　　］（　　　　　　　　　　）
4. consume...（〜を摂取/消費する）

　　　　　　　　　　　　　　―― consumption ［　　　　　］（　　　　　　　　　　）
5. excel...（〜より秀でる、〜を超える）

　　　　　　　　　　　　　　―― excellent 　　［　　　　　］（　　　　　　　　　　）
6. aggressive（積極的な）　　―― aggressively ［　　　　　］（　　　　　　　　　　）

Key Expressions 3

SVOC という文型の C は目的補語と呼ばれ、目的語(O)に情報を付加する役割を持っています。特に目的補語が不定詞になるときは、目的語の行う行為の説明をしています。日本語訳を参考に、1〜3の（　　）内に当てはまる動詞を選択肢から選び、書き入れましょう。

1. The manager of the student cafeteria wants students to (　　　　　　　　　　　　　)
   interested in each other's cultural cuisines.
   その学生食堂の店長は、学生たちにお互いの食文化に興味を持ってもらいたいと考えている。

2. Being able to eat certified halal food in the cafeteria enables the student to
   (　　　　　　　　　　　　) spare time otherwise spent cooking for studying.
   学生食堂でハラール認証された食品を食べることができることは、その学生がさもなければ（学生食堂でハラールだと認証された食品を食べることができなければ）料理に費やされる空き時間を勉強に使うことを可能にする。

3. The University of Miyazaki has opened the Islamic Center where Muslim
   students are allowed to (　　　　　　　　　　) and gather.
   宮崎大学は、イスラム教徒の学生が礼拝したり集ったりすることができるような「イスラーム文化研究交流棟」をキャンパス内に開設した。

pray　　use　　become

Background Knowledge

CD 2-18

イスラム法の下で口にすることを禁止されているものについて、英文に<u>述べられていないものを 1 ～ 4 から選びましょう。</u>

　Under Islamic law, pork and foodstuffs marked by pork-derived constituents are banned from consumption. Having dishes treated with cookware or tableware that have come into contact with pork is also prohibited.

　Muslims are not permitted to drink alcohol. Chicken and beef for human consumption must be processed in accordance with Islamic standards.

The Asahi Shimbun

Note constituent「成分」

1. 豚に由来する成分が含まれた食材
2. 豚肉に触れた調理器具や食器を使った料理
3. アルコール飲料
4. 市販の鶏肉や牛肉

Newspaper English

 同一記事内で同じ内容が繰り返される場合、冗長さを避けるために多様な表現に変える工夫がなされます。

1 ～ 3 の英文の下線部はほぼ同じ内容を表します。これらの下線部を違う表現で言い換えるために（　　）内に必要な語を選択肢から選び、書き入れましょう。ただし、大文字で始める語も小文字で与えられています。

1. The college cafeteria offers halal food for (＿＿＿＿＿＿＿＿＿) Muslim students from Islamic nations (＿＿＿＿＿＿＿＿＿) Japanese students.
   その学生食堂は、<u>イスラム諸国から来た学生にも日本人の学生にも</u>向けたハラールフードを提供している。

2. The halal food offered at the college cafeteria is popular among students from Muslim countries, (＿＿＿＿＿＿＿＿＿) Japanese students.
   その学生食堂で提供されているハラールフードは、<u>日本人の学生にもイスラム諸国から来た学生にも</u>人気がある。

3. (＿＿＿＿＿＿＿＿＿) students from Islamic countries but Japanese students can enjoy halal food at the student cafeteria.
   その学生食堂では、<u>イスラム諸国から来た学生も日本人の学生も</u>ハラールフードを食べることができる。

as well as	not only	both	and

Reading

College cafeteria offers halal food for both Muslims and Japanese

MIYAZAKI — The University of Miyazaki now offers five halal meals prepared according to Islamic traditions to all students, irrespective of whether they are Muslim.

The food offerings at the campus cater to those from
5 Indonesia, Malaysia and other Muslim countries, as well as Japanese students eager to learn about Islamic culture through the cafeteria's menu.

"Not only students from Islamic states but curious Japanese students can enjoy the delicacies," said Yoichiro
10 Yoshinaga, who manages the student restaurant. "Through the cafeteria, I want them to become interested in each other's cuisine cultures."

Among the halal specialties are chicken rendang, a curry dish featuring coconut milk, and an azuki bean paste roll
15 and two types of leavened bread. The remaining one, chicken curry, quickly ran out of stock but is now back on the menu.

The dishes were certified by the Department of Islamic Development Malaysia, also known as JAKIM. Tools to cook and dish up the food, along with materials, have been
20 recognized as halal.

A student from Indonesia studying forestry at the university's graduate school said she examines food products at stores for halal certifications when she cooks at home. She even checks the ingredient labeling of the food she purchases.
25 She said she pays special attention when eating out with Japanese students and usually opts for vegetable salads and orange juice on such occasions.

"Being able to consume certified halal food at the students' cafeteria is a great source of comfort," she said. "That enables
30 me to use spare time otherwise spent cooking for studying."

The University of Miyazaki aggressively recruits foreign students. However, numbers of students from overseas dropped significantly from a peak of 200 to 141 as of May this year due to the COVID-19 pandemic. Of that figure, 30
35 or so come from Muslim nations.

irrespective of...「~に関係なく」
cater to...「~の希望に応じる」

delicacy「珍しい食べ物」

specialty「名物料理」
chicken rendang「チキンルンダン」
leavened bread「(イースト菌を使用した) 発酵パン」
run out of stock「品切れになる」
Department of Islamic Development Malaysia「マレーシア・イスラム開発庁」
dish up...「~を盛り付ける」
forestry「森林学」
ingredient「成分」
purchase...「~を購入する」
opt for...「~を選択する」
occasion「場合」

significantly「顕著に」
as of...「~現在」

"We are creating a better life environment for students while respecting cultures from all over the world. In this way, we expect to attract excellent students from overseas," said a sectional chief at the college's Global Support Office.

40 Aside from the cafeteria, the university has opened the Islamic Center where Muslim students can pray and gather.

The Asahi Shimbun

sectional chief「係長」

Global Support Office「国際連携課」

aside from...「～とは別に」

Comprehension

本文の内容に合うように、1の質問の答えとして適当なものを、2と3の英文を完成させるのに適当なものを、a～dから選びましょう。

1. Which of the following is NOT mentioned as one of the reasons why the University of Miyazaki cafeteria began offering halal meals on its menu?
   a. To improve the quality of campus life for Muslim students
   b. To establish relationships with halal certification agencies
   c. To broaden students' perspectives when it comes to other cultures
   d. To draw international students to the university

2. The graduate student from Indonesia
   a. avoids eating at restaurants with Japanese students.
   b. takes great care to choose halal-certified products when shopping for food.
   c. was disappointed that chicken curry was temporarily unavailable at the cafeteria.
   d. prefers to spend her free time cooking rather than studying.

3. The international student population at the University of Miyazaki
   a. includes students from 30 Muslim countries.
   b. increased dramatically as a result of the COVID-19 pandemic.
   c. numbered 200 at its highest point.
   d. is not permitted to perform religious practices on campus.

Summary

DL 42　　CD 2-20

以下の空所１〜４に当てはまる語を選択肢から選び、書き入れましょう。

With the aim of initiating cultural awareness, helping Muslim students feel at home, and appealing to (1.　　　　　　　) international applicants, the University of Miyazaki has taken the step of providing a selection of officially (2.　　　　　　　) halal meals in its cafeteria. Along with the Islamic Center, this helps Muslim students feel more (3.　　　　　　　) on campus. Meanwhile, Japanese students can gain insight into international cultures while also enjoying (4.　　　　　　　) new foods

delicious　　certified　　comfortable　　potential

Insights into Today's World

DL 43　　CD 2-21

以下の対話の空所に、あなたのアイデアを書いてみましょう。その後、クラスメイトにその内容を伝えてみましょう。

I think it is important to deepen your understanding of cultural diversity when students from various cultural backgrounds are on your campus. **Besides a student cafeteria, what other ideas can you come up with for that purpose?**

How about _____

_____

Chapter 15

Competing for Cutting-Edge Robot Technology

ロボット山岳救助隊、参上

A robotic exploration vehicle (Provided by the Japan Innovation Challenge steering committee)

● Key Expressions 1

🎧 DL 44　◎ CD 2-22

音声を聞いて 1 ～ 3 の（　　）内に適当な語を書き入れましょう。

1. In the Alpine Rescue Contest 2022, a robotic exploration (v _ _ _ _ _ _) rushed
   to "rescue" a mannequin on a mountain.
   山岳遭難救助コンテスト 2022 で、ロボット探査機が山中のマネキンを「救助」するために駆け付けた。

2. The (o _ _ _ _ _ _ _ _ _) of the contest gave participants three tasks: discovery,
   delivery and rescue.
   コンテスト主催者は、出場者に「発見」「駆け付け」「救助」という 3 つの課題を与えた。

3. (P _ _ _ _) money was awarded for each successfully completed stage.
   各ステージを成功させるごとに賞金が授与された。

Key Expressions 2

名詞を修飾するハイフンでつながれた複合形容詞は、辞書に掲載されていないこともしばしばありますが、名詞の性質や特徴をはっきり示すだけでなく、切れ味の良い語調にすることもできます。

日本語訳を参考に、1～5の（　　）内に当てはまる語を選択肢から選び、書き入れましょう。

1. remote-(　　　　　　　　　　　) drones　　［遠隔操作のドローン］

2. drone-(　　　　　　　　　　) search service

　　　　　　　　　　　　　　　　　　［ドローンをもとにした捜索サービス］

3. 300-(　　　　　　　　　　) forest area　　［300 ヘクタールの森林地帯］

4. three-(　　　　　　　　　) mission　　［3 段階の課題］

5. cutting-(　　　　　　　　　) robot technology　　［最先端のロボット技術］

based　　controlled　　stage　　edge　　hectare

Key Expressions 3

1～3 は山岳遭難救助コンテストの 3 段階の課題について述べた英文です。（　　）内に当てはまる語を選択肢から選び、適当な形に変化させて書き入れましょう。

1. The first time the "discovery" stage was accomplished in time

　　(　　　　　　　　　　　　) in 2016.

　　「発見」のステージが時間内に達成されたのは、2016 年が初めてであった。

2. The bounty of the "delivery" goal was 2 million yen, and it was first

　　(　　　　　　　　　　　　) in 2017.

　　「駆け付け」の目標の賞金は 200 万円で、2017 年に初めて授与された。

　　参考　各課題の賞金額：「発見」300 万円、「駆け付け」200 万円、「救助」2,000 万円

3. As for the "rescue" goal, no team in the history of the contest

　　(　　　　　　　　　　　　) completed the process.

　　最終段階である「救出」のゴールについては、コンテストの歴史上、その過程を完遂したチームはまだない。

award　　be　　have

Background Knowledge

CD 2-23

第 5 回山岳遭難救助コンテスト 2022 で参加チームが課せられた課題内容について、英文に<u>述べられていないもの</u>を 1 ～ 4 から選びましょう。

The teams were first tasked with discovering the mannequin using drones and reporting its location and image to the contest organizer within 80 minutes of the "missing report."

They then had to deliver a 3-kilogram rescue kit to the mannequin in 30 minutes, and finally bring the rescued victim to the starting point of the contest within 300 minutes of beginning the task. *The Asahi Shimbun*

1. 最初にドローンを使ってマネキンを発見すること。
2. マネキンを発見してから 80 分以内に、その場所と画像を主催者に報告すること。
3. 主催者に報告後、30 分以内に救助キットをマネキンに届けること。
4. 最終的に 5 時間以内に救助したマネキンをスタート地点に持ち帰ること。

Newspaper English

 英文記事では、動詞の時制はニュースが起こった「時」を伝える重要な役割があります。過去のある時点に起こったことは過去時制で表します。動詞の変化に注意しましょう。

山岳遭難救助コンテストについて述べられた、以下の英文の 1 ～ 4 の（　　）内の動詞を適当な時制に書き直しましょう。

The Alpine Rescue Contest ($^{1.}$ be hold →) for the fifth time in 2022. This time, the missions ($^{2.}$ be →) more difficult than before. In the previous four contests, drones ($^{3.}$ be operate →) at the starting point located at the foot of the mountain. This time, however, contestants ($^{4.}$ operate →) them at an abandoned elementary school about 5 kilometers away.

山岳遭難救助コンテストは、2022 年に第 5 回が開催された。その課題は、以前より難易度の高いものとなった。これまでの 4 回のコンテストでは、山のふもとにあるスタート地点でドローンが操作されていた。しかし、今回、出場者は 5km ほど離れた廃校になった小学校でそれらを操作した。

Reading

Contest aims to improve robots for rescues on mountains

KAMI-SHIHORO, Hokkaido — The fifth Alpine Rescue Contest was held here, featuring the latest robots, drones and exploration vehicles that could be used to save people lost or stranded on mountains.

feature... 「〜が主役を演じる、〜を呼び物にする」
strand 「立ち往生させる」

5 "Technologies have steadily been accumulated through our contest," said Tatsufumi Kamimura, head of the event's steering committee. "We will build a system someday in which robots can quickly discover and rescue anyone and protect as many lives as possible."

steadily 「着実に」
accumulate... 「〜を蓄積する」」
steering committee 「実行委員会」

10 The Alpine Rescue Contest 2022 was held in a forested mountain area in Kami-Shihoro on Oct. 8 to 10. Four teams from in and outside Hokkaido were tested on their ability to quickly find and rescue a mannequin representing a missing hiker.

represent... 「〜に扮した」
missing 「行方不明の」

15 Organizers of the contest included a robot service provider in Tokyo and the town of Kami-Shihoro, which provided a 300-hectare forest area for the competition. In the scenario of the contest, a man picking edible wild plants goes missing, and contestants must complete a three-stage mission: 20 discovery, delivery and rescue.

edible wild plant 「山菜」

Participants deployed a variety of techniques to locate the mannequin, including the use of thermal images taken by drones with artificial intelligence. Some teams developed vertical takeoff and landing (VTOL) aircraft with fixed wings 25 that can fly longer and carry heavier loads. But only one contestant, Team ArduPilot Japan (TAP-J) from Tokyo, succeeded in locating the mannequin amid the bad weather and repeated communications failures.

deploy... 「〜を使う」
thermal image 「熱画像」
vertical 「垂直の」
load 「荷物」
communications failures 「通信障害」

Using a rover, TAP-J became the first team to reach the 30 mannequin on a steep slope below a hiking course 2 kilometers from the starting point. But the machine's battery lost voltage when it tried to lift the mannequin's legs, and the team gave up on the rescue.

steep 「急な」
voltage 「電圧」

"The slope of the mountain was difficult to confirm at some 35 points through the images sent from the rover," said Hiroshi

confirm... 「〜を確認する」

Kitaoka, 37, who headed TAP-J. "Our successful response to the slope, a fallen tree and the rough weather gave us confidence, though."

response「対応」

rough「荒れた」

The competition aims to establish certain rescue
40 technologies, including remote-controlled drones that can promptly search for missing individuals and rovers that can rush to the scene when personnel cannot be dispatched, such as at night or amid danger of secondary accidents.

establish...「～を確立する」

promptly「迅速に」

personnel「人員」

dispatch...「～を派遣する」

secondary accident「二次災害」

A drone-based night search service called Night Hawks,
45 which came out of the contest, was put into practical use last year in Hokkaido, the northeastern Tohoku region and elsewhere.   *The Asahi Shimbun*

put into practical use「実用化する」

● **Comprehension**

本文の内容に合うように、1と2の英文を完成させるのに適当なものを、3の質問の答えとして適当なものを、a～dから選びましょう。

1. The Alpine Rescue Contest 2022

    a. consisted only of Hokkaido-based organizers and participants.

    b. failed to produce a team capable of accomplishing the delivery mission.

    c. took place amid clear weather conditions.

    d. asked teams to rescue a local man who went missing on the mountain.

2. Team ArduPilot Japan decided to give up the rescue mission due to

    a. fallen trees which made the slope impassable.

    b. power issues after the rover attempted to lift the mannequin.

    c. bad weather conditions which damaged their machine's batteries.

    d. repeated communications failures with their rover.

3. Which is NOT an advantage of the types of technologies the competition aims to establish?

    a. The ability to locate missing individuals with greater speed

    b. The capability to operate amid dangerous conditions

    c. The potential for greater monetary profit than human-based rescue strategies

    d. The means to perform rescue operations at night

Summary

🎧 DL 45　◎ CD 2-25

以下の空所 1 ～ 4 に当てはまる語を選択肢から選び、書き入れましょう。

The Alpine Rescue Contest 2022 featured teams showcasing
(¹.   ) rescue technologies as they attempted to
complete their mission. Deploying vehicles, such as drones and rovers, which
were equipped with various tools, including (².   )
imaging, teams were tasked with recovering a mannequin located in a
(³.   ) area in Hokkaido where the contest was
held. The competition encourages the development of innovative rescue
techniques that can be utilized in (⁴.   ) rescue
scenarios.

thermal　　cutting-edge　　forested　　real-world

Insights into Today's World

🎧 DL 46　◎ CD 2-26

以下の対話の空所に、あなたの質問を書いてみましょう。その後、クラスメイトにその内容を伝えてみましょう。

It's wonderful that the results of the rescue contests have led to practical applications like the Night Hawks. **What do you think about rescue robots becoming a reality?**

I'm very excited about it because ＿＿＿＿＿＿＿＿＿＿＿＿＿＿＿＿＿＿＿＿＿＿

However, I'd be worried ＿＿＿＿＿＿＿＿＿＿＿＿＿＿＿＿＿＿＿＿＿＿＿＿＿＿＿＿＿

Chapter

16

Can You Do Without It?

手放すことで学ぶこと

Josh Spodek shows the empty refrigerator in his Greenwich Village apartment (AP / Aflo)

● Key Expressions 1

🎧 DL 47   ◎ CD 2-27

音声を聞いて 1 〜 3 の（　　）内に適当な語を書き入れましょう。

1. Josh Spodek is living (s _ _ _ _ _ _ _ _ _) in New York City by unplugging his refrigerator.

   ジョシュ・スポデック氏は、ニューヨーク市で彼の冷蔵庫のプラグを抜いて持続可能な生活を送っている。

2. The fridge was the biggest (s _ _ _ _ _) of electricity usage in his Greenwich Village apartment.

   冷蔵庫が、彼の住むグリニッジ・ヴィレッジのアパートメントでの電力使用の最大の原因だった。

3. He (v _ _ _ _) it as unnecessary for everyone to keep their refrigerators running all the time.

   彼は、すべての人が冷蔵庫を四六時中動かしておく必要がないと考えている。

101

Key Expressions 2

1 ～ 6 は本文に出てくるフレーズです。日本語を参考に、（　　　）内に適当な語を選択肢から選び、書き入れましょう。

1. give (　　　　　　　　　　) flying 　　　　　［飛行機に乗るのをやめる］
2. go (　　　　　　　　　　) a refrigerator 　　［冷蔵庫なしで済ませる］
3. identify the fridge (　　　　　　　　　　) the biggest source of electrical use
　　［冷蔵庫が電力の使用の最大の原因だと突き止める］
4. be (　　　　　　　　　　) risk 　　　　　　［危険な状態にある］
5. be (　　　　　　　　　　) refrigeration 　　［冷蔵に反対である］
6. cancel (　　　　　　　　　) the energy savings　［エネルギーの節約を相殺する］

at　　against　　out　　without　　up　　as

Key Expressions 3

日本語訳を参考に、1 ～ 3 の英文の（　　）内に適当な接続詞を選択肢から選び、書き入れましょう。ただし、文頭に来る語も小文字で与えられています。

1. (　　　　　　　　　) he's climbing the stairs, he thinks about people around the world who live without modern amenities.
彼は階段を登っているとき、現代の生活に便利なものなしに生きる世界中の人たちのことを考える。

2. Through this act, he is learning more about their cultures than (　　　　　　　　　) he just flew in for a week.
この行為を通じて、彼は、ただ一週間どこかに飛行機で行った場合よりも、その人たちの文化についてより多くを学んでいる。

3. Now he just has to eat what he buys (　　　　　　　　　) it goes bad or pickle it so it lasts a bit longer.
今では彼は購入したものを腐る前に食べたり、少し長持ちさせるために漬物にしたりしなければならないだけである。

if　　before　　when

Background Knowledge

CD 2-28

冷蔵庫を持たない節約生活をしているアメリカ人のスポデック氏について、英文に<u>述べら</u>
<u>れていないもの</u>を1～4から選びましょう。

Beyond the energy savings, Spodek — who works as an executive coach, teaches leadership as an adjunct professor at New York University, and blogs and podcasts about his experiences — says that going fridge-free has improved his quality of life. He buys fresh produce at farmers' markets, receives boxes of produce from a farm cooperative (CSA, or community-supported agriculture), keeps a stock of dried beans and grains, and has become adept at some fermentation techniques.

He cooks with an electric pressure cooker and, very rarely, a toaster oven, powering them with a portable solar panel and battery pack. *The Associated Press*

Notes adjunct professor「非常勤教授」 produce「農産物」 grain「穀物」 become adept at...「～に熟達する」
fermentation「発酵」

1. ニューヨーク大学で教鞭をとりながら、経営陣のコーチとしても働いている。
2. 生産者のマーケットで新鮮な野菜や果物を購入している。
3. 料理をするときは電気圧力鍋しか使わない。
4. 携帯用ソーラーパネルやバッテリーパックを使って電力を得ている。

Newspaper English

 英文記事のインタビューのコメントなどでは、I thought that.... などと従属節を含んだ英文が用いられることがありますが、主節の動詞が過去時制の場合、基本的には従属節内の（助）動詞も過去形になり時制の一致が起こります。

1と2の英文の（　　）内の助動詞を適当な形に直しましょう。

1. I didn't really have a plan for how I (will →　　　　　　　　　　) get by without one.
   冷蔵庫なしにどうやってしのげばいいのか、私は本当のところ無計画だった。

2. But I figured it (will not →　　　　　　　　　　) kill me, and I (can →　　　　　　　　　　) always plug in the fridge again.
   でも、それで死ぬわけではないし、またいつだって冷蔵庫の電源は入れられると私は思った。

Reading

A fridge too far? Living sustainably in NYC by unplugging

NEW YORK — There are those for whom recycling and composting are not nearly enough, who have reduced their annual waste to almost zero, ditched their clothes dryer or given up flying, and are ready to take the next step in exploring the frontiers of sustainable living.

For Manhattanite Josh Spodek, that has meant going without a refrigerator, which he identified as the biggest source of electricity usage in his Greenwich Village apartment.

Spodek began by deciding to go packaging-free, and one small step led to another. Now, he is living virtually grid-free in a city that in many ways is the epitome of grids.

"It was a mindset shift followed by continual improvement," Spodek says. He first unplugged the fridge for three winter months, and then the next year for around six months (from November to early spring, when food generally kept for about two days on his windowsill). Now, he's been fridge-free for over a year.

Spodek is quick to point out that he's not against refrigeration in general, but views it as unnecessary for everyone to have one running 24/7. In many parts of the world, he notes, refrigerators are a rarity.

"People in Manhattan lived without refrigeration until the mid-20th century," he says, "so it's clearly doable."

Critics are quick to point out that this experiment should not be taken lightly.

"People's lives can be at risk if certain foods go off. Certain dairy products go off very easily and quickly if you're not careful," says Frank Talty, founder and president of the New York-based Refrigeration Institute, which trains students to install and service refrigerators and air conditioners.

When he first unplugged his fridge, Spodek says, "I honestly wasn't sure I could survive a week without it. I didn't really have a plan for how I would get by without one. But I figured it wouldn't kill me, and I could always plug it

---

compost「堆肥を作る」

ditch...「〜を処分する」

frontier「未開の地」

virtually「事実上」

grid-free「送電網の不要な」

in many ways「多くの意味において」

epitome「縮図」

mindset「考え方」

windowsill「(窓の下枠部分にある)窓台、窓の下枠」

24/7「24時間年中無休で」

note「述べる、指摘する」

rarity「めったにないもの、稀なもの」

doable「実行可能な、することができる」

go off「腐る」

dairy product「乳製品」

Refrigeration Institute (=The Air-Conditioning, Heating, and Refrigeration Institute) 米国空調暖房冷凍工業会

service...「〜を修理する」

get by「なんとかやっていく」

in again."

Being a vegan without the need to refrigerate meat or dairy products certainly helps.

vegan「菜食主義者」

Skeptics — and there are many — point out that going
40 without a refrigerator requires near-daily food shopping. For those with large families or who need to drive to get groceries, more frequent shopping trips could cancel out the energy savings.

skeptic「懐疑的な人」

Not to mention, the inconvenience would be untenable for
45 most.

inconvenience「不便、不便であること」

Also, improvements to fridges over the years mean they typically use less power now than, say, a heating system or water heater.   *AP News*

untenable「擁護できない」

Comprehension

本文の内容に合うように、1 と 2 の英文を完成させるのに適当なものを、3 の質問の答えとして適当なものを、a 〜 d から選びましょう。

1. Josh Spodek

a. takes a strong stance against going packaging-free.

b. began living sustainably by first giving up his clothes dryer.

c. survives by storing meat on the windowsill of his Manhattan apartment.

d. took a gradual approach toward becoming refrigerator free.

2. One reason why Spodek believed refraining from the use of refrigerators was possible was because

a. there are many regions in the world where people don't use refrigerators.

b. it is possible to refrigerate food naturally throughout the year.

c. most modern refrigerators use less power than older models.

d. the technology was not used until the late 20th century.

3. Which is NOT a disadvantage of giving up refrigerators mentioned in the text?

a. It may be necessary to increase frequency of food shopping.

b. It is inconvenient for most people.

c. Vegans might find it particularly challenging.

d. There is a risk of consuming spoiled food.

● Summary

以下の空所1～4に当てはまる語を選択肢から選び、書き入れましょう。

After discovering the amount of electricity his refrigerator (1.   ), Manhattan resident, Josh Spodek, decided to give up use of the appliance altogether. While he (2.   ) that this lifestyle is not for everyone, he nonetheless (3.   ) that people tend to use their refrigerators more than necessary and that living without them is possible. Counterarguments include the inconvenience this would cause for large families and that in some cases, adapting to life without a refrigerator (4.   ) out any energy savings.

consumes   cancels   acknowledges   argues

● Insights into Today's World

DL 49 CD 2-31

以下の対話の空所に、あなたのアイデアを書いてみましょう。その後、クラスメイトにその内容を伝えてみましょう。

Did you know about this man living without a fridge in New York? I can't imagine going without one, but we should probably do something like that in order to save our earth. **What do you think you can do to cut use of electricity?**

That's an important question. Maybe it would be possible for me to _____

_____

Chapter 17

An Apocalypse Already in Progress

消えゆく虫と生態系の未来

Fireflies in a glass jar (Aflo)

Key Expressions 1

 DL 50　　 CD 2-32

音声を聞いて 1 ～ 3 の（　　）内に適当な語を書き入れましょう。

1. When he was a boy in the 1960s, David Wagner would run around his family's farm with a glass jar (c _ _ _ _ _ _ _) in his hand and scoop flickering fireflies out of the sky.

   1960 年代に少年だったころ、デイビッド・ワグナー氏は、彼の家族所有の農場を、片手にガラス瓶を握りしめ、空からチカチカと光る蛍をすくって捕まえようと走り回ったものだ。

2. His beloved fireflies have largely (v _ _ _ _ _ _ _) in what scientists are calling the global insect apocalypse.

   彼のこよなく愛する蛍は、科学者たちが世界的な昆虫の大惨事と呼んでいる状況の中、大幅に消滅してしまっている。

3. With fewer insects, we would have less food and see (y _ _ _ _ _) of all crops dropping.

   昆虫が少なくなれば、私たちは食料が減り、すべての農産物の収穫高が減るだろう。

Key Expressions 2

1〜5は虫の行動に関する語句です。日本語訳を参考に、（　　　）内に適当な語を選択肢から選び、書き入れましょう。

1. (　　　　　　　　　　　　　) through rainforest canopy　［熱帯雨林の林冠を這う］
2. (　　　　　　　　　　　　　) into soil　　　　　　　　　　［土に潜り込む］
3. (　　　　　　　　　　　　　) freshwater ponds　　　　　［淡水の池の水面をすれすれに飛ぶ］
4. (　　　　　　　　　　　　　) through the air　　　　　　　［空中をひらひらと飛ぶ］
5. (　　　　　　　　　　　　　) rangeland soil　　　　　　　［放牧場用地の土をかき混ぜる］

Note　canopy「林冠（森林の上層部の、高木の枝葉が覆い茂った部分のこと）」

> skim　churn　burrow　flit　crawl

Key Expressions 3

日本語訳を参考に、1〜3の英文の（　　　）内の動詞を適当な分詞（-ed, -ing）にしましょう。

1. Wagner's family farm is now paved over with new homes and (manicure
   →　　　　　　　　　　　　　　　) lawns.
   ワグナー氏の家族の農場は今では新しい家や、綺麗に刈り込まれた芝生に覆われている。

2. Insects are the fabric (tether →　　　　　　　　　　　　　) together every
   freshwater and terrestrial ecosystem across the planet.
   虫たちは地球中のあらゆる淡水や土の生態系を繋ぎとめている骨組みである。

3. Insects pollinate more than 75% of global crops, a service (value →
   　　　　　　　　　) at up to $577 billion per year.
   虫たちは世界の農作物の75%以上を受粉させ、それは年間最大で5,770億ドルの価値を持つ作業である。

Background Knowledge

CD 2-33

虫と動物界との関係について、英文に述べられていないものを 1 〜 4 から選びましょう。

In terms of diversity, insects are unrivaled, representing two-thirds of the world's more than 1.5 million documented animal species with millions more bugs likely still undiscovered, scientists said. By comparison, there are roughly 73,000 vertebrates, or animals with a backbone, from humans to birds and fish — these represent less than 5% of the known Animal Kingdom, according to the International Union for Conservation of Nature (IUCN).

Insects' importance to the environment can't be understated, scientists said. They are crucial to the food web, feeding birds, reptiles and mammals such as bats. For some animals, bugs are simply a treat. Plant-eating orangutans delight in slurping up termites from a teeming hill. Humans, too, see some 2,000 species of insects as food.

Reuters

Notes vertebrate「脊柱動物」 understate...「〜を少なく言う」 reptile「爬虫類」 mammal「哺乳類」 treat「ごちそう」 slurp「チューチュー食べる」 termite「シロアリ」 teeming hill「シロアリのたくさんいるアリ塚」

1. まだ発見されていない可能性のある虫はおそらく何百万種といる。
2. 国際自然保護連合によると、存在する約 73,000 種の脊柱動物は、既知の動物界の 5% 弱を占める。
3. 虫は、食物連鎖にとって重要で、鳥、爬虫類、コウモリのような哺乳類を養っている。
4. オランウータンは、約 2,000 種の虫を食料としている。

Newspaper English

英文記事には読者の知らない専門用語が使われることも多いです。その際、ダッシュ（–）や同格のコンマ（,）などを使って読者の理解を補う情報が盛り込まれることも多く、理解を助けてくれます。

日本語を参考に、1 〜 3 の（　）内に適当な語を選択肢より選び、必要であれば形を変えて書き入れましょう。

On the biological "tree of life" — which (1.　　　　　　　　　) organisms to describe their evolutionary and genetic relationship to one another — insects (2.　　　　　　　　　) under the branch, or phylum, (3.　　　　　　　　　) arthropods, one of the 40 branches of the animal kingdom.

進化的および遺伝的な相互関係を述べるために生物を分類する生物学上の「生命の樹」においては、虫は、動物界の 40 の部門の内のひとつである、節足動物と呼ばれる分科あるいは門に入る。

call　　fall　　classify

Reading

From fireflies to dung beetles, insects are vanishing

As a boy in the 1960s, David Wagner would run around his family's Missouri farm with a glass jar clutched in his hand, scooping flickering fireflies out of the sky.

"We could fill it up and put it by our bedside at night,"
5 said Wagner, now an entomologist.

That's all gone, the family farm now paved over with new homes and manicured lawns. And Wagner's beloved fireflies — like so many insects worldwide — have largely vanished in what scientists are calling the global insect
10 apocalypse.

As human activities rapidly transform the planet, the global insect population is declining at an unprecedented rate of up to 2% per year. Amid deforestation, pesticide use, artificial light pollution and climate change, these
15 critters are struggling — along with the crops, flowers and other animals that rely on them to survive.

It's easy to think insects are doing OK. After all, they're nearly everywhere — crawling through rainforest canopy, burrowing into soil, skimming freshwater ponds or, of
20 course, flitting through the air.

On the biological "tree of life" — which classifies organisms to describe their evolutionary and genetic relationship to one another — insects fall under the branch, or phylum, called arthropods, one of the 40
25 branches of the animal kingdom.

"Insects are the food that make all the birds and make all the fish," said Wagner, who works at the University of Connecticut. "They're the fabric tethering together every freshwater and terrestrial ecosystem across the planet."

30 But insects are so much more than food. Farmers depend on these critters to pollinate crops and churn soil to keep it healthy, among other activities.

Insects pollinate more than 75% of global crops, a service valued at up to $577 billion per year, the
35 Intergovernmental Science-Policy Platform on Biodiversity

dung beetle「フンコロガシ」

entomologist「昆虫学者」

unprecedented「前例のない」
deforestation「森林伐採、森林破壊」
pesticide「殺虫剤」
critter「生き物、虫」
struggle「もがく」

110

and Ecosystem Services (IPBES) says.

In the United States, insects perform services valued in 2006 at an estimated $57 billion per year, according to a study in the journal *BioScience*.

40 Dung beetles alone are worth some $380 million per year to the U.S. cattle industry for their work breaking down manure and churning rangeland soil, the study found.

With fewer insects, "we'd have less food," said ecologist Dave Goulson at the University of Sussex. "We'd see yields of 45 all of these crops dropping."

And in nature, about 80% of wild plants rely on insects for pollination. "If insects continue to decline," Goulson said, "expect some pretty dire consequences for ecosystems generally — and for people."

Reuters

cattle industry「畜産業」

manure「厩肥（きゅうひ、家畜の糞尿や草などを含む肥料）」

rangeland「放牧場」

dire「悲惨な」

consequence「状況」

参考

The Intergovernmental Science-Policy Platform on Biodiversity and Ecosystem Services (IPBES)「生物多様性及び生態系サービスに関する政府間科学政策プラットフォーム」

● **Comprehension**

本文の内容に合うように、1と3の英文を完成させるのに適当なものを、2の質問の答えとして適当なものを、a～dから選びましょう。

1. David Wagner

  a. is an ecologist at the University of Connecticut.

  b. grew up on a farm in rural America.

  c. specializes in the study of fireflies.

  d. coined the term, 'insect apocalypse.'

2. Which of the following is NOT an example of human activity that is causing a decline in the global insect population?

  a. chemical treatment of crops

  b. excessive use of unnatural light sources

  c. using machines to churn rangeland soil

  d. large-scale clearing of forested land

3. The global insect population

    a. has declined by 80% since the 1960s.

    b. is surging at a rate of 2% annually.

    c. can be divided into 40 branches.

    d. pollinates over 75% of the world's crops.

● Summary   🎧 DL 51   ◉ CD 2-35

以下の空所 1 ～ 4 に当てはまる語句を選択肢から選び、書き入れましょう。

> Among the consequences of human activity plaguing the (1.   ) is the startling decline of the insect population. Given their (2.   ) as a food source for other animals across Earth's ecosystems, as well as their valuable role in pollination and soil treatment, a (3.   ) of this trend will have dangerous repercussions. For one thing, the decline of the insect population will lead to a (4.   ) in crop yields, which means less food for people.

decrease   continuation   importance   planet

● Insights into Today's World   🎧 DL 52   ◉ CD 2-36

以下の対話の空所に、あなたのアイデアを書いてみましょう。その後、クラスメイトにその内容を伝えてみましょう。

> I remember that many years ago, I stayed at my grandma's house and caught so many fireflies. But I didn't see even one this summer. I'm worried that they are quickly vanishing from the earth. **Have you noticed any changes when it comes to insects recently?**

I noticed that _____

_____

Tailoring Tea to Taste

留学生とのコラボで日本茶を世界へ

Ryutaro Matoba, left, and Abhishek Gupta (Provided by Yomoyama Inc.)

Key Expressions 1

🎧 DL 53　　◎ CD 2-37

音声を聞いて 1 ～ 3 の（　　）内に適当な語を書き入れましょう。

1. In recent years, both the (p _ _ _ _ _ _ _ _ _) and export of green tea have been on the rise.

   近年、緑茶の生産量、輸出量ともに増加してきている。

2. Fennel seeds are (w _ _ _ _ _) used as a mouth freshener in India.

   フェネルシードは、インドでは口内清涼剤として広く用いられている。

3. Hojicha is roasted after the tea leaves are (s _ _ _ _ _ _).

   ほうじ茶は、茶葉が蒸気で蒸された後に焙煎される。

Key Expressions 2

接頭辞 sub- は「〜の下の」、「〜の下位の」、「副〜」などの意味を持ちます。

1 〜 5 の日本語の意味になるように、選択肢より適当な語を選び、接頭辞 sub- を付けて（　　）内に書き入れましょう。

1. 下位範疇　　　　　　　　（　　　　　　　　　　　　　）
2. 下位文化　　　　　　　　（　　　　　　　　　　　　　）
3. （小説などの）わき筋　　（　　　　　　　　　　　　　）
4. 亜大陸　　　　　　　　　（　　　　　　　　　　　　　）
5. 潜在意識の　　　　　　　（　　　　　　　　　　　　　）

亜大陸：大陸の中で地理的に独立した広い一部分

> plot　　conscious　　continent　　category　　culture

Key Expressions 3

「make ＋動詞の名詞形」からなる熟語は数多く、頻繁に用いられます。基本的なものは、使いこなせるようにしておきましょう。日本語訳を参考に、1 〜 3 の（　　）内に当てはまる語を選択肢から選び、書き入れましょう。

1. The man is in charge of making (　　　　　　　　　　) to the tea production
   process.
   その男性は、茶の製造工程に改良を加える責任者である。

2. Gupta and Matoba made blending (　　　　　　　　　) to make
   Japanese tea easy to drink for people overseas.
   グプタさんと的場さんは、海外の人々にも日本茶を飲みやすくするための配合を試した。

3. They made final (　　　　　　　　　) based on advice from other
   foreign students.
   彼らは他の留学生からのアドバイスに基づいて最終決定をした。

> attempts　　improvements　　decisions

● Background Knowledge

CD 2-38

海外における日本茶市場について、英文に述べられているものを 1 ～ 4 から選びましょう。

　People in the U.S. are said to be drinking more Japanese tea and less alcoholic beverages. Many cafes in the U.S. — as well as Asia and Europe — have added matcha teas to their menus. Demand is expected to continue to grow. According to market research firm Global Information Inc., the global market for matcha alone was worth $2.75 billion in 2021 and is predicted to reach $4.28 billion in 2027.

The Japan News

1. アメリカ合衆国では、アルコール飲料に日本茶を混ぜて飲む人が増えている。
2. ヨーロッパとは違い、アメリカでは多くのカフェが抹茶をメニューに加えた。
3. 2021 年の抹茶の世界市場規模は、27 億 5 千万ドルであった。
4. 2027 年の抹茶の世界市場規模は、4 億 2,800 万ドルに達すると見込まれている。

● Newspaper English

 代名詞としての other の使い方は、対象が 2 つに限定されているか、3 つ以上かによって異なります。また、the を付けて用いる場合は「残りのすべてのもの」を指しますが、the を付けずに others とする場合は、いくつかあるもののうち「残りのいくつか」という意味になります。

日本語訳を参考に、1 と 2 の英文の（　　）内に入るものを選択肢から選び、書き入れましょう。

1. They have made two kinds of blended Sayama tea. One is cinnamon-flavored "hoji-cha" tea and (　　　　　　　　　　　　) is green tea blended with fennel seeds.
　彼らは 2 種類のブレンド狭山茶を作りました。ひとつはシナモン風味のほうじ茶で、もうひとつはフェネルシードをブレンドした煎茶です。

2. We have three foreign students in our class. One is from Sweden and (　　　　　　　　　　　) are from India.
　私たちのクラスには 3 人の留学生がいます。ひとりはスウェーデンからの留学生で、残りの 2 人はインドからの留学生です。

the others　　others　　the other

Reading

Tea farmer eyes India as export market with cinnamon flavor

Shipping Japanese green tea to India, one of the world's top tea-drinking nations and a major exporter of Assam and Darjeeling tea, would seem on the face of it to make little sense. Yet, Ryutaro Matoba, a Sayama tea farmer, reckons
5 he has found the perfect formula to appeal to the vast market that the subcontinent offers.

Matoba credits his good fortune to Abhishek Gupta, a student from India who advised him to flavor the leaves with cinnamon and fennel seeds, spices popular in his home
10 country.

Matoba befriended Gupta, who studies environmental sciences at the University of Tokyo's Graduate School, through a socializing event in January 2022. The session was organized by Yomoyama Inc., which supports companies
15 seeking to crack open overseas markets and also assists foreign students studying in Japan.

Seven students from six countries, including Brazil, Turkey and Malaysia, attended the event. While they talked with Matoba online and visited his plantation, the students
20 shared ideas to make Sayama tea popular in their home countries.

Gupta's proposal to export tea tailored to local tastes to India won the most support from the participants. A crowdfunding campaign raised more than 600,000 yen for
25 the project, exceeding the goal of 500,000 yen.

Gupta came to Japan seven years ago, and he was struck by the health properties of Japanese green tea. Chai, a type of milk tea containing heaps of sugar, is consumed across India. He imagined Japanese green tea could prove popular
30 in his home country if it was flavored with spices that Indians like.

Seeking advice from other foreign students, Gupta and Matoba made blending attempts to make tea easy to drink for people overseas. Two products got the seal of approval in
35 November 2022. One is cinnamon-flavored "hoji-cha" roasted

---

eye... 「〜を見つめる、注視する」

exporter 「輸出国」

on the face of it 「一見したところ、表面上は」

make little sense 「ほとんど意味がない」

reckon... 「〜と考える」

formula 「調合、製法」

credit... to 〜 「(功績など)を〜のおかげとする」

good fortune 「幸運」

flavor... 「〜に風味をつける」

befriend... 「〜と友人になる」

environmental science 「環境科学」

socializing 「社交的な交際(交流)」

organize... 「〜を企画する、組織する」

crack open... 「〜を切り拓く」

plantation 「農園」

tailor to local tastes 「地元の人の好みに合わせる」

raise... 「(資金など)を集める」

exceed... 「〜を上回る、〜を超える」

be struck by... 「〜に感銘を受ける」

property 「特徴」

heap of... 「山のような〜、たくさんの〜」

get one's seal of approval 「(人の)承認(お墨付き)を得る」

tea and the other is green tea blended with fennel seeds.

"Both Japanese and foreign nationals can enjoy the flavors," Matoba said. "We will keep making improvements to create a blend of tea that will be cherished for a long time."

cherish...「～を愛する、大切にする」

The Asahi Shimbun

Comprehension

本文の内容に合うように、1と3の質問の答えとして適当なものを、2の英文を完成させるのに適当なものを、a～dから選びましょう。

1. How did Ryutaro Matoba and Abhishek Gupta initially meet?
   a. They were classmates at the University of Tokyo.
   b. Through a gathering involving international students.
   c. They both attended an event at the Yomoyama Inc. headquarters.
   d. While Matoba was visiting a tea plantation in India.

2. By blending it with certain spices, Abhishek Gupta believes that Japanese tea can
   a. taste better than chai tea.
   b. gain popularity in the Indian tea market.
   c. have increased health benefits.
   d. prove more popular than Assam or Darjeeling tea.

3. Which of the following did NOT play a role in supporting Gupta's proposal?
   a. the Graduate School of Arts & Sciences at Tokyo University
   b. a company that supports international students studying in Japan
   c. students from various countries
   d. funds donated via a crowdfunding campaign

● Summary

🎧 DL 54　◎ CD 2-40

以下の空所 1 ～ 4 に当てはまる語を選択肢から選び、書き入れましょう。

Sayama tea farmer, Ryutaro Matoba and graduate student, Abhishek Gupta have formed a (1.   ) with the aim of bringing Japanese tea to Gupta's home country of India. Because of the health benefits of Japanese green tea, Gupta believed it could appeal to tea (2.   ) in India. The flavor, however, does not suit Indian (3.   ), so Matoba and Gupta have produced (4.   ) of tea that are more likely to be appreciated.

blends　　drinkers　　tastes　　partnership

● Insights into Today's World

🎧 DL 55　◎ CD 2-41

以下の対話の空所に、あなたのアイデアを書いてみましょう。その後、クラスメイト
にその内容を伝えてみましょう。

I am impressed with the idea of exporting Japanese tea to India. There might be other traditional Japanese products that could be popular overseas. **What do you think might be another candidate?**

Perhaps _____

_____

Stuart Fowkes records the sound of a passing London Underground train. (AFP-Jiji)

● Key Expressions 1

🎧 DL 56   ◉ CD 2-42

音声を聞いて 1 〜 3 の（　　）内に適当な語を書き入れましょう。

1. Field recording, put simply, is the act of recording the sounds of an (e _ _ _ _ _ _ _ _ _).

   フィールド・レコーディングとは、簡潔に言えば、ある環境の音を録音する行為である。

2. Mr. Fowkes has been thrilled by the (r _ _ _ _ _ _ _) to his project.

   フォークスさんは、彼のプロジェクトに対する反応にわくわくしている。

3. The "obsolete sounds" project is the world's largest (c _ _ _ _ _ _ _ _ _) of obsolete and disappearing sounds.

   「失われつつある音」プロジェクトは、世界最大の失われつつある消えゆく音のコレクションである。

Key Expressions 2

building や meeting などのように語尾が -ing(s) の名詞があります。1 〜 5 の日本語の意味を持つ語を選択肢から選び、(　　) 内に書き入れましょう。

1. スケッチ、図面　　　　　(　　　　　　　　　　　　)
2. 研究成果、調査結果　　　(　　　　　　　　　　　　)
3. 録音　　　　　　　　　　(　　　　　　　　　　　　)
4. 周囲の状況　　　　　　　(　　　　　　　　　　　　)
5. 予約　　　　　　　　　　(　　　　　　　　　　　　)

> booking(s)　　surrounding(s)　　recording(s)　　finding(s)　　drawing(s)

Key Expressions 3

日本語訳を参考に 1 〜 3 の英文の ［　　］ 内の語句を正しい語順に並べ替えましょう。なお、文頭に来る語も小文字で与えられています。

1. [make / anyone / a decent recording / can] on their smartphone.
   だれでも自分のスマートフォンで、きちんとした録音ができる。

   _____

2. New sounds are appearing faster [in / than / at / time / any] history.
   新しい音が今史上最速で現れている。

   _____

3. We will be glad [any / answer / questions / to] about this project.
   このプロジェクトに関するどのような質問にも喜んでお答えいたします。

   _____

Background Knowledge

(◉) CD 2-43

ロンドンの地下鉄や、その音を録音しているフォークスさんについて、英文に述べられているものを1〜4から選びましょう。

Moving below street level down into London's Underground train network, Mr. Fowkes gets to work again.

A bit like the "trainspotters" who were once a familiar sight on the platforms of UK railway stations, Mr. Fowkes is a dedicated "soundspotter".

But to him, there is nothing dull or uninteresting about the screeching of the train's wheels scraping against the curves in the metal tracks or the clunk of the doors opening and closing.

AFP-Jiji

Notes trainspotter「鉄道マニア」 screeching「キーッという音」 scrape against...「〜をこする」 clunk「ガチャンという音」

1. ロンドンの地下鉄のプラットフォームでは今でも鉄道マニアをよく見かける。
2. フォークスさんは、熱心な「音マニア」であると同時に鉄道マニアでもある。
3. 車輪が線路のカーブをこするキーッという音は、フォークスさんにとってあまり興味深くはない。
4. 地下鉄車両のドア開閉時のガチャンという音は、フォークスさんにとっては全然退屈ではない。

Newspaper English

英文記事では、過去の出来事を目の前で起こっているように生き生きと描写するために、現在形を用いることがあります。見出しだけでなく、記事の本文にも見られますので注意しておきましょう。

日本語訳を参考に、1と2の英文の（　　）内に入る語を選択肢から選び、書き入れましょう。

1. Mr. Fowkes (　　　　　　　　　　) out a hand-held recording device and
   (　　　　　　　　　) into action.
   フォークスさんは携帯型録音機器をさっと取り出し、即座に行動に移す。

2. Mr. Fowkes (　　　　　　　　) the sound of a passing London Underground train at Blackfriars tube station in London.
   フォークスさんはロンドンの地下鉄ブラックフライヤーズ駅で通り過ぎるロンドン地下鉄車両の音を録音する。

swings　　records　　whips

Reading

UK project aims to preserve lost sounds

The mostly defunct red phone boxes no longer attract much attention in London except from tourists. But Mr. Stuart Fowkes is thrilled to stumble upon one still in working order.

5　Its ring is one of the world's disappearing noises that his pioneering "obsolete sounds" project is dedicated to preserving.

He whips out a hand-held recording device and swings into action, explaining, "I've always had sonic curiosity.

10　"New sounds are appearing faster than at any time in history, but they are also changing and disappearing faster than ever before."

His latest project aims to preserve sounds that are "just on the edge of memory".

15　These sounds that we are "just about forgetting" are the ones that have the "greatest emotional resonance", he said.

"What I have been struck by is how people have responded emotionally to some of the recordings.

"You've got people who heard the sound of a Super 8 film 20　camera and this reminded them of being in their living room in 1978 with their dad showing them home movies for the first time."

The "obsolete sounds" project features more than 150 recordings collected from around the world, and also includes 25　remixes of those sounds by musicians and sound artists.

Billed as the biggest collection of its kind, it includes everything from Walkman personal stereo cassette players and old video game consoles, to steam trains and vintage racing cars, as well as sounds that evoke the rapidly 30　changing natural environment, such as crumbling glaciers.

"Before the industrial revolution, our sound environment would not have changed much for hundreds of years," says Mr. Fowkes.

"Today, the pace of change is ridiculous. Things that are 35　only a few years old, like ring tones on mobile phones, already sound dated."

preserve...「～を保存する」

defunct「機能していない」

stumble upon...「～を偶然見つける」

in working order「（機械などが）正常に動作する状態で」

ring「電話のベルの音、着信音」

pioneering「先駆的な」

be dedicated to...「～に専念する」

sonic curiosity「音への興味」

on the edge of...「～の端に、～の瀬戸際で」

just about doing「今にも～しようとしている」

emotional resonance「情緒的共鳴」

be struck by...「～に感銘を受ける」

Super 8 film「スーパー 8 フィルム、スーパー 8 mm フィルム（1965年に発表された個人映画向けのムービーフィルムの規格）」

remind ... of ～「…に～を思い出させる」

remix「リミックス（複数の既存曲を編集して新たな楽曲を生み出す手法の一つ）」

billed as...「～といわれる」

steam train「蒸気機関車」

vintage「年代物の」

evoke...「～を連想させる、想起させる」

crumble「崩れる、砕ける」

glacier「氷河」

ridiculous「どうかしている」

dated「時代遅れの、古くさい」

The digital consultant launched Cities and Memory in 2015 and has drawn in some 1,000 collaborators across the globe.

draw in...「〜を集める」
collaborator「協力者」

"Every morning I wake up to emails with recordings from
40 somewhere completely unexpected, like a beach in Bali or even the metro in Pyongyang."

Anyone can contribute, he says, just by "sticking their mobile phone out of the window" and then visiting citiesandmemory.com.   *AFP-Jiji*

stick ... out of 〜「…を〜から突き出す」

Comprehension

本文の内容に合うように、1と3の英文を完成させるのに適当なものを、2の空所に当てはまる答えとして適当なものを、a 〜 d から選びましょう。

1. The "obsolete sounds" project aims to preserve sounds

    a. that have disappeared from the world.

    b. of the world's various modern cityscapes.

    c. created by musicians and sound artists.

    d. which are on the brink of being forgotten.

2. According to Stuart Fowkes, some people had a ____ response upon hearing the sound of a Super 8 film camera.

    a. pathetic

    b. resentful

    c. nostalgic

    d. bitter

3. Fowkes' website, "Cities and Memory,"

    a. focuses on collecting the local sounds of London in the UK.

    b. features more than 150 recordings from around the world.

    c. accepts contributions from the general public.

    d. compiles exclusively urban-based sounds.

Summary

以下の空所 1 ～ 4 に当てはまる語を選択肢から選び、書き入れましょう。

In response to the rapidly changing sound environment of the (1.   ) world, digital consultant Stuart Fowkes has established the "obsolete sounds" project. The aim of the project is to collect and preserve a (2.   ) variety of sounds that are in danger of disappearing. With recordings that range from the mundane to the (3.   ), Fowkes has observed that some have the potential to elicit a (4.   ) response from the listener.

wide　　modern　　fantastic　　sentimental

Insights into Today's World

DL 58　CD 2-46

以下の対話の空所に、あなたのアイデアを書いてみましょう。その後、クラスメイトにその内容を伝えてみましょう。

As Mr. Fowkes says, all sorts of sounds are now disappearing so fast and without anyone even noticing. **What kind of sounds would you like to preserve?**

As for me, _____

_____

124

Chapter 20

New Leadership at Harvard University

アメリカの名門大学が創る新たなリーダー像

Incoming Harvard University president, Claudine Gay (Stephanie Mitchell/Harvard University/AFP/Aflo)

Key Expressions 1

🎧 DL 59　　◎ CD 2-47

音声を聞いて1〜3の（　　）内に適当な語を書き入れましょう。

1. Claudine Gay will be Harvard University's second female president after (f _ _ _ _ _) president Drew Faust.

クローディン・ゲイ氏は、ドリュー・ファウスト前学長に続くハーバード大学の二人目の女性学長となる。

2. There are (r _ _ _ _ _ _ _ _) few U.S. universities that are led by Black presidents.

黒人の学長が率いるアメリカの大学は、比較的少ない。

3. In her speech, Gay expressed her excitement and (g _ _ _ _ _ _ _) for being elected president.

スピーチの中で、ゲイ氏は学長に選出されたことに対する興奮と感謝を表明した。

Key Expressions 2

ある一つの単語の語形が変化してできた単語のことを派生語と呼びます。品詞の異なる派生語をまとめて覚えておくと、効率的に語彙を増やすことができます。

以下の1〜5の名詞の日本語訳をa〜eから選び、[　　]内に書き入れましょう。
またそれぞれの単語の動詞の原形を（　　）内に書き入れましょう。

1. announcement 　　[　　] 　（　　　　　　　　　　）
2. introduction 　　[　　] 　（　　　　　　　　　　）
3. participation 　　[　　] 　（　　　　　　　　　　）
4. collaboration 　　[　　] 　（　　　　　　　　　　）
5. appointment 　　[　　] 　（　　　　　　　　　　）

a. 参加　　b. 紹介　　c. 任命　　d. 協力　　e. 発表

Key Expressions 3

日本語訳に合うように、1〜3の英文の（　　）内に適当な副詞を選択肢から選び、書き入れましょう。

1. Gay (　　　　　　　　　　) serves as the Edgerley Family Dean of Harvard's Faculty of Arts and Sciences.
   ゲイ氏は現在、ハーバード大学芸術科学部のエッジャリー・ファミリー学部長を務めている。

2. She is (　　　　　　　　　) humbled by the prospect of leading that incredible institution.
   彼女は、その素晴らしい機関を率いることの期待に、非常に恐縮している。

3. This presidential hire will (　　　　　　　　　　) be one of the most significant in American higher education for years to come.
   この学長採用は、今後数年間、アメリカの高等教育でほぼ間違いなく最も重要なものの一つになるでしょう。

incredibly　　currently　　arguably

Background Knowledge

CD 2-48

ローレンス・バコウ氏がハーバード大学の第 29 代学長として就任していた時の状況について、英文に<u>述べられていないもの</u>を 1 ～ 4 から選びましょう。

Lawrence Bacow, who took over as president in 2018, expanded and updated the university's teaching and research missions and fostered cooperation across disciplines to address issues including climate change and inequality.

Under his leadership, Harvard joined the Massachusetts Institute of Technology in a legal challenge to the Trump administration's decision to make international students leave the country if they planned on taking classes entirely online in fall 2020 at the height of the pandemic. He criticized the policy for its "cruelty" and "recklessness."

AP News

Note discipline「学問分野」

1. ローレンス・バコウ氏は、2018 年にキャンパスを拡張した。

2. 同氏は、気候変動や不平等などの問題に取り組むため、分野間の協力を促進した。

3. 2020 年の秋学期、完全オンラインで授業を受けることを計画している留学生を国外に退去させるという政権の決定がなされた。

4. 同氏は、政権の政策を「残酷」で「無謀」だと批判した。

Newspaper English

 Chapter 6 で学習したように、英文記事の中で、人物のコメントはしばしば直接話法で紹介されます。直接話法を間接話法に書き換える際の主なステップは、次の通りです。

① 主節の動詞を伝達動詞（tell, ask など）に変える
② 被伝達部を that 節に変える
③ 被伝達部の中に使われる代名詞を（必要に応じて）適切なものにする
④ 被伝達部の動詞の時制を適切な形にする

例：He said to her, "I'm going to Osaka." → He told her that he was going to Osaka.

1 と 2 の直接話法の英文を間接話法に書き換えましょう。

1. She said to me, "I am absolutely humbled."

   → She told _____ .

2. He said to us, "Claudine will be a remarkable leader."

   → He told _____ .

Reading

Claudine Gay to be Harvard's 1st Black president, 2nd woman

Harvard University announced that Claudine Gay will become its 30th president, making her the first Black person and the second woman to lead the Ivy League school. Gay, who is currently a dean at the university and a democracy
5 scholar, will become president July 1. She replaces Lawrence Bacow, who is stepping down and has said he wanted to spend more time with family.

"This is crazy, right?" a beaming Gay said as she was introduced to applause at the Smith campus center. She
10 currently serves as the Edgerley Family Dean of Harvard's Faculty of Arts and Sciences. "I am absolutely humbled by the confidence that the governing board has placed in me," she said. "I am also incredibly humbled by the prospect of succeeding President Bacow and leading this incredible
15 institution."

A child of Haitian immigrants, Gay is regarded as a leading voice on the issue of American political participation. Among the issues she has explored is how a range of social and economic factors shape political views and influence
20 voting choices. She also is the founding chair of Harvard's Inequality in America Initiative, which studies issues like the effects of child poverty and deprivation on educational opportunity and American inequality from a global perspective.

25 In her speech, Gay called for greater collaboration among schools at Harvard and said there was an urgency for the university to be more engaged with the world and to "bring bold, brave and pioneering thinking to our greatest challenges."

30 Gay will be the only Black president currently serving in the Ivy League and the second Black woman ever, following Ruth Simmons, who led Brown University from 2001 to 2012. Gay's appointment is remarkable in part because relatively few U.S. universities are led by Black presidents,
35 said Eddie R. Cole, a historian of college presidents and race

lead... 「〜を率いる」

Ivy League「アイビーリーグ（アメリカ名門 8 大学の総称）」

democracy「民主主義」

step down「退任する」

beaming「喜びに満ちた」

applause「拍手喝采」

absolutely「完全に」

confidence「信頼」

governing board「理事会」

immigrants「移民」

regard as... 「〜とみなす」

voice「発言者」

explore...「〜を探求する」

voting「選挙」

poverty「貧困」

deprivation「剥奪」

perspective「視点」

urgency「緊急」

be engaged with...「〜と関わる」

bold「大胆な」

brave「勇敢な」

remarkable「注目に値する」

at the University of California, Los Angeles. Harvard wields outsized influence in higher education, he said, and other universities are bound to take notice.

40 "At a time when everyone continues to look at Harvard, this presidential hire will arguably be one of the most significant in American higher education for years to come," Cole said.

AP News

wield... 「(影響力など) を持つ」

outsized 「非常に大きな」

be bound to... 「～するにちがいない」

hire 「採用」

significant 「重要な」

● Comprehension

本文の内容に合うように、1 と 3 の英文を完成させるのに適当なものを、2 の質問の答えとして適当なものを、a ～ d から選びましょう。

1. Claudine Gay will become

  a. the first Black person and the first woman to be president of an Ivy League school.

  b. Harvard's second Black president.

  c. the first woman to become dean of Harvard's Faculty of Arts and Sciences.

  d. the Ivy League's only current Black president.

2. Which of the following topics is not connected to Claudine Gay's academic pursuits?

  a. inequality in America

  b. child deprivation

  c. illegal immigration

  d. formation of political views

3. In her speech at the Smith campus center, Claudine Gay called for Harvard University to

  a. collaborate with other schools to solve problems.

  b. wield its influence in the world of higher education.

  c. use innovative thinking to confront serious challenges.

  d. consider American inequality from a global perspective.

Summary

🎧 DL 60   💿 CD 2-50

以下の空所 1 ～ 4 に当てはまる語を選択肢から選び、書き入れましょう。

Claudine Gay, a (1. _____) academic in the field of political science, has been announced as the next president of Harvard University. Her appointment is significant as she will be the first Black woman to serve as president of the (2. _____) institution, and only the second in the history of the Ivy League schools. As (3. _____) U.S. universities are led by Black presidents, it is possible that other schools will be influenced by this (4. _____) decision and will follow Harvard's lead when it comes to choosing a president.

few   prestigious   distinguished   momentous

Insights into Today's World

🎧 DL 61   💿 CD 2-51

以下の対話の空所に、あなたの考えを書いてみましょう。その後、クラスメイトにその内容を伝えてみましょう。

A person of color will lead Harvard University for the first time in its nearly 400-year history. **What do you believe society can do to eliminate the prejudice faced by historically oppressed people?**

I believe that _____

_____

Acknowledgements

All the news materials are reprinted by permission of The Asahi Shimbun, The Mainichi, Kyodo News[+], The Japan News, Reuters, The Japan Times, The New York Times, and AFP-Jiji.

TEXT CREDITS

Chapter 01   Hug a Seal, Begin to Heal

This adorable robot therapy seal helps relieve anxiety, stress

The Asahi Shimbun, December 16, 2022 (partially modified)

Chapter 02   Inheriting Traditional Sounds

Shamisen industry in a pinch to protect unique sound integral to Japanese theater

The Mainichi, January 1, 2023 (partially modified)

Chapter 03   Used Home Appliances Gaining Popularity

Market for used home appliances undergoes a sea change in Japan

The Asahi Shimbun, November 17, 2022 (partially modified)

Chapter 04   The Ideal Solid Fuel

Japanese firms look to plant-based, carbonneutral "biocoke" fuel to cut CO_2 emission

The Mainichi, June 19, 2022 (partially modified)

Chapter 05   Dress Codes to Promote Gender Equality

Banks changing with the times by ditching female-only uniforms

The Asahi Shimbun, December 30, 2022 (partially modified)

Chapter 06   Do You Dare Take the "Train to Apocalypse"?

Jakarta train firm holds 'zombie' event to scare up more passengers

Kyodo News[+], October 4, 2022 (partially modified)

Chapter 07   Island Doctor Saves the Day

Telesurgery may soon be practical option in Japan

The Japan News, May 23, 2022 (partially modified)

Captivated by island, doctor relocates to treat residents

The Japan News, November 12, 2022 (partially modified)

Chapter 08   Changing Flavor with Magic Tableware

What's cooking with Japanese developer's "magic tableware" that changes taste?

The Mainichi, January 21, 2023 (partially modified)

Chapter 09   Rethinking Our Relationship with Animals in Captivity

Zoos move to reduce stress for animals in their care

The Japan News, September 18, 2022 (partially modified)

本書にはCD（別売）があります

Insights 2024
世界を読むメディア英語入門2024

2024年1月20日　初版第1刷発行

編著者　　村　尾　純　子
　　　　　深　山　晶　子
　　　　　辻　本　智　子
　　　　　横　山　香　奈
　　　　　Christopher Cladis

発行者　　福　岡　正　人
発行所　　株式会社　金星堂

（〒101-0051）　東京都千代田区神田神保町 3-21
Tel　（03）3263-3828（営業部）
　　　（03）3263-3997（編集部）
Fax　（03）3263-0716
https://www.kinsei-do.co.jp

編集担当　蔦原美智、長島吉成　　　　　　　　Printed in Japan
印刷所・製本所／萩原印刷株式会社

ISBN978-4-7647-4192-8　C1082